THE REFORM OF ELEMENTARY SCHOOL EDUCATION

THE REFORM OF ELEMENTARY SCHOOL EDUCATION

A Report on Elementary Schools in America and how they can Change to Improve Teaching and Learning

by
Frank Brown, Ed.D

KRIEGER PUBLISHING COMPANY
MALABAR, FLORIDA
1992

Original Edition 1992

Printed and Published by
KRIEGER PUBLISHING COMPANY
KRIEGER DRIVE
MALABAR, FLORIDA 32950

Copyright © 1992 by Krieger Publishing Company

All rights reserved. No part of this book may be reproduced in any form or by any means, electronic or mechanical, including information storage and retrieval systems without permission in writing from the publisher.
No liability is assumed with respect to the use of the information contained herein.
Printed in the United States of America.

Library of Congress Cataloging-in-Publication Data

Brown, B. Frank (Bartley Frank), 1917–
    The reform of elementary school education: a report on elementary schools in America and how they can be changed to improve teaching and learning / by B. Frank Brown.—Original ed.
    p. cm.
    Includes index.
    ISBN 0-89464-475-0 (alk. paper)
    1. Education, Elementary—United States—Evaluation.
2. Elementary schools—United States. 3. School improvement programs—United States. 4. Educational change—United States.
I. Title.
LA219.B76   1991   91-7282
372.973—dc20   CIP

10 9 8 7 6 5 4 3 2

For
Kate, Robin, Louis, Stuart
Sterling, and Catherine

THE MISSION

The nation's elementary schools have failed to make the connection between our lifestyle, our national security, our economy, our technology, and the quality of education. In an initiative designed to make elementary school education more vigorous, and at the same time appropriate to the changing demography of the nation, this report describes the mission and how it can be accomplished.

CONTENTS

Introduction   xi

CHAPTER 1   1
A Nation In Jeopardy

CHAPTER 2   19
Demography Of The Elementary Schools In The 1990's

CHAPTER 3   27
Elementary Education In The 1990's

CHAPTER 4   47
Dilemmas Of The Elementary Schools' Curricula

CHAPTER 5   63
A Reform Response To The Learning Deficit

CHAPTER 6   75
How To "Guarantee" Student Achievement

CHAPTER 7   91
Significant Issues In Improving Student Outcomes

CHAPTER 8   105
The Cause Of The Decline In Learning And What
To Do About It

CHAPTER 9   115
The Case For Curricular Reform In Elementary Schools

CHAPTER 10   133
The Case For And Against Educational Technology:
An Elusive Reform

Contents x

CHAPTER 11 141
Executive Summary Of Recommendations For
Elementary School Reform

References 149

Index 153

Introduction

Each generation has the opportunity to shape education in its time. The task of the present generation differs from previous periods in that after centuries of progress our system of elementary education is stagnant. Meanwhile, the rapid changes in the structure of the American family and changing gender roles present a challenge not previously encountered by elementary schools.

A volatile mismatch now exists between the product of the schools and the needs of the nation. For all intents and purposes the present system of schooling has failed, leaving the nation with an alarming learning deficit. The task of reforming education has become more complex because, while American education was faltering, the world became increasingly more competitive and intellectually challenging, moving beyond the capabilities of the schools. The rapid changes in society and the world at large have simply outstripped the ability of the nation's elementary schools to adapt. They have faced so many crises that they now suffer from crisis fatigue.

To be specific, the inability of teachers to teach mathematics and science well in the elementary schools is in marked contrast to what is happening in other industrialized countries. The issue is one that affects the quality of our technological advancement in this decade and ultimately our national defense. Unless we solve the problem of giving children a firm foundation in math and science, the nation will lose long-range high technology leadership.

The gap between the complex needs of industry and what

schools can deliver has widened to catastrophic proportions. It is time to recognize that the quality of education for our children puts a limit an everything we can accomplish as a nation.

When he made his first report card on the nation's schools, Secretary of Education Lauro Cavazos concluded that student performance is now "stagnant," a sobering indictment. The secretary further commented, "This situation scares me and I hope it scares you, too." He then disclosed his profound concern with the statement: "We must do better or perish as the nation we know today." (Press Release, Department of Education 7/88)

Because of poor schooling our children are literally in a crisis. Elementary schooling for many is a nightmare due to the misfit between what the schools offer and what the children need. The crisis for the children is very real, and a reaction of righteous anger from an indulgent society is long overdue. As one disconcerted third grader commented to the author about his frustration with school, "My nightmares all come in the daytime."

The nation's system of public schools is in serious trouble. The parade of reports documenting its ills seems endless. Their impact has been to agitate a great deal of turmoil both within the education community and from other interested and affected groups. The debate at the elementary school level over appropriate responses to an institution suffering from obsolescence has been surprisingly benign. There has been very little finger pointing. This is probably a result of the fact that until quite recently the education establishment has managed to keep relatively tight control over the agenda of the debate, and in an institution as bureaucratized and complex as education it is difficult to target a villain.

The problem is that the numerous efforts at reform have been more fragmented than cohesive. We have had a plethora of suggestions but no comprehensive plan. Secretary Cavazos diagnosed the problem as a lack of overall direction.

Throughout the 1980's schools sandbagged most reform efforts by halfheartedly introducing haphazard and piecemeal reforms. These lukewarm efforts miserably failed to increase students' dreadfully inadequate reading and writing skills. This unsystematic approach to reform can no longer be indulged.

Introduction xiii

Society has been remarkably patient with the schools, but to continue to be patient, when the schools have clearly failed in their mission and are not educating vast numbers of children, is downright foolish, if not outright criminal. The time is past for writing new scenarios for reform. It is a time for indignation and action.

The dismal record of the schools can no longer be justified by the people who run them or tolerated by the people who fund them. The shortfall in learning is so serious that business, for the first time in history, is becoming heavily involved with the schools, claiming to be "the educator of last resort."

The nation's learning deficit has laid the groundwork for a new trend in American education in which the power to operate and control education is shifting from local authorities to state policy makers. The wresting of power from local school districts is happening because the public has lost confidence in the ability of local school boards to educate the nation's children. This action coincides with a public perception that schools are not in tune with society. What is most needed in the elementary schools is a clear voice of reason in a noisy room of confusion and disorder.

The shift in power is not as dramatic as it seems at first blush. The notion that the governance of schools is a local matter is no more than a popular myth. For a number of years the states have increased their allocation of funds for education, and with this increase in support has come some alteration in governance. But it is now time to recognize that the states and federal government have legitimate and responsible roles to play in financing education, setting standards, and imposing policy.

In response to the nation's disappointing performance in international economic competition, the National Governor's Association has led the charge for a consensus on a new national resolve to reshape education.

The centerpiece for this new reform effort is the premise that now is a time for results. The outcomes sought for the elementary schools are significant improvements in achievement in the areas of reading, mathematics, science, geography, and history.

To attain the results that are needed, policy makers now

believe that educators must be held personally responsible and accountable for the learning of students in their charge. Those who cannot produce advances in student performance should be replaced by others who can. In the past, accountability measures have been applied to schools but with no visible progress. Accountability is a clean word and a concept which is well understood, but it works only when applied to the performance of individuals. It cannot pertain to institutions.

In addition to concentrating on results, the educational reform agenda must reevaluate the issue of who is allowed into the teaching profession. The colleges of education are incapable of rethinking their mission, and at present most teacher education programs accept any warm body who walks in off the street. For the past decade teachers have been coming from the bottom of the academic barrel and the schools have been considered little more than an enterprise like the postal service or the telephone company where anybody can perform the job.

The shameful levels of student performance that characterize American elementary education are no longer acceptable. The schools have never bothered to figure out what it is they want the product of our education system to look like. No specifications have been developed for the product we want educational production to yield. Passive inaction can no longer be endured. Forceful action and spectacular changes are required if we are to attain impressive gains in student performance. A burgeoning consensus confirms that educational reform is an urgent matter which can best be led and directed by the governors and state policy makers.

CHAPTER 1

A Nation In Jeopardy

The school reform movement in America began when the National Commission on Excellence in Education (1983) warned:

> The nation is at risk. . . . The educational foundations of our society are presently being eroded by a rising tide of mediocrity that threatens our very future as a nation and a people.

The report served notice that both society and its schools,

> have lost sight of the basic purpose of schooling and of the high expectations and disciplined effort needed to attain them.

Although nine years have passed and the sounding of the alarm was loud and clear, America has failed to address the risk. Mediocrity in schooling and the decline in learning have continued and are accelerating. The result is a nation in jeopardy.

What has come to pass in the eight year interval since the Commission on Excellence warned of impending catastrophe if the schools failed to improve? A lot of noise has been made about reform and the states have pumped huge amounts of new money into schools, but nothing has really changed. Educators have not responded to the challenge, and student performance has improved only marginally. School critics are becoming increasingly frustrated, and many now contend that putting more money into our failed schools is a foolish extravagance. They opt for reforming the system from the ground up.

A consequence of the lack of progress is a plethora of reports condemning the shameful levels of performance that characterize Americas education. Some call for revisions in curriculum, others for change in the structure of schools; some cite deficiencies in the way teachers are educated, while others examine signs of decay in the social and economic structures of society. On one point they all agree: the schools must be reformed.

By any objective standard evaluative criteria, public education is a failure. This is now admitted by even the various teachers' unions and civil rights groups. The basic goal of educating all children up to their best level of ability remains no more than a distant dream. And now the schools should be embarking on a new mission to enable each student to develop capacities for a lifetime of learning and for meaningful participation in an increasingly diverse society.

INTERVENTION BY THE PRESIDENT

In an attempt to stem the "rising tide of mediocrity," President Bush called an unprecedented Education Summit with the nation's governors in September, 1989. His purpose: to energize the issue of reform and to improve the nation's elementary and secondary schools. (White House Press Release 2/26/90).

In his summit address to the governors, the President deplored the lack of progress in education and asserted that the United States "lavishes unsurpassed resources" on the education of its children.

Shortly after the summit, White House Domestic Policy Advisor Roger Porter met with the National Conference of State Legislatures and reported that the nation was spending "more per capita" and "more per student," in comparison to education spending in other countries.

These declarations about lofty expenditures for elementary and secondary education caused quite a brouhaha a short time later, when the Washington based Economic Policy Institute released spending data flatly contradicting the declarations of the president and his domestic policy advisor that the country spends more on education than its economic rivals. The Economic Policy Institute's paper asserted that the U.S. actually spends far less on elementary and secondary education than thirteen other major industrialized nations. ("Shortchanging Education," January 1, 1990).

Among other conclusions, the release by the Institute maintained that the size of the nation's financial commitment to education was exaggerated by the inclusion of spending for higher education in the international comparisons. The report asserted that this incorporation of higher education expenditures "obscures the main focus of concern about American education deficiencies in the elementary and secondary schools."

The Institute's study used data from the National Center for Education Statistics and the United Nations Educational, Scientific and Cultural Organization to compare the U.S. financial effort in education with the expenditures of Canada, Japan, Australia, and twelve Western European nations.

Using analytic methods which, its authors claim, allowed more valid comparisons than other research to date, the study ranked the United States fourteenth among countries studied in the percentage of national and per capita income spent on K-12 education. Only Australia and Ireland expended lesser amounts.

In Congress, Chairman of the House Education Committee Augustus F. Hawkins expressed alarm over the Institute's findings. "The study graphically confirms that our national commitment to educating young people remains more rhetorical than real. It is embarrassing to see the U.S. in the bargain basement of education support when compared internationally." (*Education Week* 1/24/90).

The issue of more money for schools is moot. Teachers salaries have now reached a national average of $33,000 for 196 days of work. For the number of day's work the salaries are comparable to those of most professions. If teachers are to be paid more, they should work a longer year. Increased support is imperative for improvement in curriculum and better inservice training for teachers. Additional funds are also essential for teaching assistants to reduce class size.

A LEARNING SHORTFALL

Much of the furor over the poor showing of American students on international examinations comes from the business sector, which is worried about the long range effect on the national economy. But concern for the quality of schooling must go far beyond the issues of economics and production. Education provides the strength and moral fibre of society. Individuals who fail to develop their mental powers and attain basic skills become disenfranchised and destined to live on the margin of society, unable to participate fully in our national life.

School reform becomes a new imperative when we acknowledge that the economic sovereignty formerly enjoyed by the United States has already declined drastically. The public is being made increasingly aware that other nations are now producing superior products. Furthermore, we are dealing with highly motivated competitors who have surpassed our educational attainments. With interest and anxiety mounting on several fronts, the business community is particularly distressed that our economy and position in the world are under constant challenge from the new and excellent products being developed by scientists and engineers from countries which place a higher premium on education. The states, once bystanders to international events, are becoming major players in the global market place because of their responsibility for education.

It is now generally recognized that the nation is being menaced by a quiet crisis as damaging as drugs and terrorism. The crisis is homegrown; simply put, it is the failure of the public education system. The shortfall in learning is frightening and the trend is worsening. Indications are that we will lose even more educational ground. Census Bureau data shows that if the current trend towards mediocrity continues, by the year 2000, 70 percent of the U.S. population will be functionally illiterate and consequently unemployable in modern technological society (*Education Week* 2/10/90. Defined, functional literacy is the acquisition of those skills and knowledge which enable an individual to successfully perform the survival skills needed as an adult. Minimum literacy requires being able to read at grade level 8.5, in order to understand directories, newspaper advertisements, maps, measurements of an area, etc.

FIXING HIGH SCHOOLS IS THE WRONG APPROACH

Beginning with the publication of A *Nation At Risk*. governors of all fifty states initiated a new wave of educational reform. But these initiatives, as well as the fifty research reports which followed calling for school reform, have all been flawed. Looking for a quick fix, they focused on improving the nation's high schools while the elementary schools continued to languish in mediocrity.

The school reform movement has now reached the point of overkill in the myriad exhortations for the reform of secondary education, while ignoring the alarming status quo in traditional elementary education. The result is a terrifying sameness in elementary schools. By doing what they have always done, the schools are not meeting the needs of a changing society. It is time for educators to acknowledge that more of the same is not nearly enough.

Radical reform in the elementary and middle schools, where 70 percent of the nation's children are enrolled, must now become the nation's highest educational priority. It is abundantly clear that putting the emphasis at the secondary school level where students are nearing completion of their public school education is not going to bring about massive school improvement. While there is no easy solution to the schools' shortfall in learning, developing a strategy to strengthen elementary education is a necessary first step.

Americans tend to be impatient; they want instant results and immediate solutions to problems. But that is not going to happen in education. Initiating reforms at the kindergarten and primary level will require years before the outcome of more competent high school graduates will be reached. It is imperative that we begin at the pre-kindergarten level and concentrate on rigorously teaching reading and mathematics throughout the system. The quick fixes applied at the high school level are no more than band aids on a severely wounded school system. In addition, in schools as in business, trying to fix something is more complicated and expensive than getting it right in the first place.

RESTRUCTURING, AN INCONSEQUENTIAL CHANGE

Widely discussed at the Education Summit was the notion of restructuring, one of the president's favorite ideas for changing the schools. His advisors are misguided in having him support this scheme. Education, like other professions, has its share of buzz words. These are words which are bandied about in nearly every professional conversation while in vogue, then suddenly disappear, while another buzz word takes their place. Restructuring is the current catchword in education; however, few educators actually can describe what it means. The term is vague, nebulous, and frequently used by educators who want to appear to be on top of things but have no intention of making changes. The very meaning of the word "restructuring" applied to education is elusive and varies with the person to whom one is talking.

Evidence of confusion among educators over the use of this term was substantiated at the 1990 convention of the American Association of School Administrators, an organization made up of the nation's school superintendents. Administrators flocked to the session on what restructuring was all about, but the press reported widely that most left more confused than when they arrived.

After two days of talks at a Baltimore meeting on restructuring, called by the Education Commission of the States, the Commission Chairman President Frank Newman remarked: "There's a feeling that we have been marching down the path of restructuring but without really knowing where we are going or how we get there." Another participant commented, "Crafting a vision of restructuring that is simple and compelling is the biggest barrier to change" (*Education Week* 2/21/90).

A more precise, clean-cut descriptive term for changing

the schools is "reform." While this word may seem uncompromising to some, there must be no compromise on the initiative to change schools. The solution is not "restructuring" the educational system. This implies only reasonably gentle partial changes. The system needs to be dismantled and completely reformed.

QUOTABLE QUOTES FROM THE EDUCATIONAL SUMMIT

While the Education Summit of 1989 did not accomplish much, it was an excercise in high visibility for the schools. It drew national attention to their plight and the necessity for reform to improve the quality of education. Among noteworthy statements made at the Summit were the following: (White House Press Release 2/26/90)

Governor Gerald Baliles
Chairman, National Governors' Association

> These are times for us to open our eyes and our minds and face the facts. The world has changed more than we sometimes would prefer. The challenges, both internally and externally, are profound and difficult. And frankly, we have not made it easy for ourselves.
>
> It may be said of the American federal system of government that the whole remains less than the sum of the parts. Education is one example, but not the only one. In other words, if we are to take on education as a nation, we had better get all the parts in accord and pulling together.
>
> There is a federal role to be more clearly defined, supported and sustained. In response to international economic competition, a consensus is emerging for an American national resolve. The Jeffersonian belief that education is the first, best hope for our Republic's enduring success has not diminished. We have simply discovered that as the times change, so must our ideas.

Governor Terry Branstead, Iowa
Chairman-Elect, National Governors' Association.

This is a time for results. We are working hard to achieve results in our states. Results like better student performance on math, science and foreign language tests, lower dropout rates and higher graduation rates, improved adult literacy, skilled and productive workers for the jobs of the 21st century. It is time to find new measures of performance based on what students know and what students can do; not just the number of classes that they complete in high school or college.

Lauro Cavazos, Secretary of Education

Thomas Jefferson, our first education president, was a relentless advocate for universal public education. After two centuries of progress, we are stagnant. While millions of Americans read for pleasure, millions of others don't read at all.

The National Assessment of Educational Progress estimates that fewer than one in four of our high school juniors can write an adequate, persuasive letter and only half can manage decimals, fractions and percentages. And barely one in three can locate the Civil War in the correct half-century. No modern nation can long afford to allow so many of its sons and daughters to emerge into adulthood ignorant and unskilled. The status quo is a guarantee of mediocrity, social decay and national decline.

Six years ago the Committee on Excellence in Education issued its powerful report: and yet today our nation is still at risk.

From this day forward, let us be an America of tougher standards, of higher goals and a land of bigger dreams.

Many parents have come to view education as a service we can hand over to the school boards, in much the same way we expect our cities to provide electricity or water.

There is more to learning than just our trade balance or the graying of our work force; it is broader than the important, but narrow, compass of economics and government.

THE LESSER SUMMIT

After the Education Summit, the governors returned to their various states and initiated mini-summits at the state level for the purpose of obtaining grass roots input on what to do about the education debacle.

A second and much less publicized meeting between the president and the governors was held at the White House barely five months after the Education Summit for the purpose of agreeing on a set of national goals designed to radically improve education.

The second conference opened with comments from Governor Terry Bransted of Iowa, Chairman of National Governors' Association, who declared, "It is not acceptable to just let American education sit where it is today. We are here to create a national consensus to make education world class." (National Governors' Assn. 1990).

The chief item on the agenda was a discussion of the six broad national goals worked out by the White House staff after analyzing the suggestions sent by the governors following the states' mini-summits. The national goals agreed upon for improving American education and confirmed by President Bush in his State of the Union address are as follows:

GOAL 1: By the year 2000, all children in America will start school ready to learn.

GOAL 2: By the year 2000, the high school graduation rate will increase to at least 90 percent.

GOAL 3: By the Year 2000, American students will leave grades four, eight and twelve having demonstrated competency in challenging subject matter including English, mathematics, science, history, and geography; and every school in America will ensure that all students learn to use their minds well, so they may be prepared for responsible citizenship, further learning, and productive employment in our modern economy.

GOAL 4: By the year 2000, U.S. students will be first in the world in science and mathematics achievement.

GOAL 5: By the year 2000, every adult American will be literate and will possess the knowledge and skills necessary to compete in a global economy and to exercise the rights and responsibilities of citizenship.

GOAL 6: By the year 2000, every school in America will be free of drugs and violence and will offer a disciplined environment conducive to learning. (National Governors' Association 1990)

WHY THE NATIONAL GOALS CANNOT BE REACHED

The statements of new national goals for education, like *A Nation At Risk* and the other reform reports, fail to emphasize and pinpoint specific goals and significant programs for improving the nation's elementary schools. Until elementary education is completely reformed, the nation's entire education system will continue to waste away in a sea of mediocrity.

Further, while the goals which the White House Conference set are in some ways commendable, they are overly ambitious, unrealistic, and unattainable. First, the nation's teaching corps is not up to the job. Performance of educators on the Scholastic Aptitude Test of the College Board is at the bottom of all of the professions. Even more alarming is the fact that the average S.A.T. scores of people now in training to be teachers are far below the average scores of high school students.

It should be noted that the children who, "by the year 2000 will be first in the world in science and mathematics achievement," are already in the fourth grade. Yet, no strategy has been devised for reforming the elementary schools or improving the teaching of science and mathematics. Seventy percent of all the nation's children are in grades K though 8; without a massive effort in this area, the notion of making U.S. students "first in the world in mathematics and science by the year 2000" is no more than a distant and unattainable vision. Nor can the dropout rate be reduced from 30 percent to 10 per-

A Nation in Jeopardy

cent and all Americans made literate in nine short years. The new national goals simply fail to take into consideration the sheer complexity of an enterprise as confused and decentralized as American schooling.

Up front, it must be noted that students' performance has improved little in the past twenty years, despite the fact that the states have pumped billions of dollars into school improvement plans. Focused against the schools' track record of the past twenty years, the new national goals are pie in a very distant sky.

Another disturbing issue is that the gaps in performance between white and minority students have not been bridged. White thirteen-year-olds continue to out-perform black seventeen-year-olds in math and science.

Declines continue in the proportion of students who can reason and solve problems. Before schools can fulfill the national goal of "increasing substantially" the number of students who can do these things, they must first stem the downward trend of fewer students acquiring these skills.

Hard evidence that the new national goals are too visionary for a troubled school system is contained in the first-ever state by state assessment of student achievement released in mid-1991. Student performance in mathematics varies widely among the states, but achievement in all states is embarrassingly low. For example, the assessment found that nationwide more than a quarter of the fourth graders lack the ability to perform simple arithmetic reasoning with whole numbers. Only 5 percent of the nation's high school seniors demonstrated skills needed for college-level work.

Secretary of Education Lamar Alexander described the assessment as the most comprehensive analysis ever conducted and said it should sound "an alarm bell that should ring all night throughout the country" (*Education Week* 6/21/91).

In the entire history of the nation there has never before been a common assessment of learning state by state. The prevailing sentiment in the past was not to display in public the strengths or weaknesses of schools in the various states. The results of the assessment, according to the report show quite clearly and in some detail that mathematics education in our nation and in our states is far from the vision described in the recommendations for reform of what mathematics education should be (The State Mathematics Achievement, 1991).

Perplexing researchers is the absence of changes in learning by gender. Consistently, female students outperform male students in writing and reading and males outperform females in science and math. Differences have not changed in the past two decades.

While research is clear that "hands on" learning is more effective in elementary schools than seatwork and lectures, surveys consistently report that more than 90 percent of the nation's classrooms are dominated by lectures and seatwork. There will be no notable improvement in elementary education until students are taught in the context of situations, activities, and problems.

History is replete with the failure of both the nation's and the states' past attempts to achieve education goals. The nation also set goals for education after the launching of Sputnik and during the war on poverty. None of these was achieved and they have long since been forgotten. In 1957, President Eisenhower's Commission on National Goals set as an educational goal the teaching of Chinese in "many of the nation's high schools within three to five years." Ten years later a national survey found only two high schools teaching Chinese and one of these was in the Chinatown area of San Francisco where Chinese had been taught for many years (U.S. Department of Education, 1967).

In response to *A Nation At Risk* President Ronald Reagan presented a set of four national goals in 1984. One of these goals was to raise the high school graduation rate from 70 percent to 90 percent by 1990. The graduation rate has not improved, and President Reagan's other three national goals faded from public memory well before the time set for reaching them.

A flagrant example of failure to attain state goals is the case of the former governor of Florida Bob Graham and the Florida State Board of Education. In 1982 they adopted, with much fanfare, the goal of making "educational achievement in Florida in the upper quartile of states within five years" (Florida State Board of Education Minutes 1/20/81). Eight years later, instead of improving, Florida's students had declined in achievement and scored below the national average on the Scholastic Aptitude Test.

Past experience shows that previous goal-setting efforts have been mostly rhetoric and if the nation continues to set goals which are not even remotely met, then educational improvement is dead in the water. The practice of setting goals without a tough strategy for achieving them raises false hopes and at the same time diverts attention from the hard question about why our education system is in such poor shape.

After the president and governors agreed on national goals for the nation's education system, the rest of the White House discussions revolved around a series of educational platitudes about a society dedicated to an educational renaissance and about students who are now average achieving by the year 2000 what our best students are achieving now. The platitudes are as irresponsible and unattainable as the new national goals. Schools cannot be reformed by proclamation.

At the federal level, the next step is for the president and the governors to adapt visible mechanisms for reaching the targeted goals. These should include a detailed action plan and annual progress reports on the efforts to reach the goals. Without reports on progress, the goals will remain illusory rhetoric.

If America's educational performance is to be markedly improved, significant and major reforms must be expeditiously initiated and supported in elementary education. This basic and primary part of the educational system has been ignored for too long by state and national policy makers.

A COMPREHENSIVE REFORM STRATEGY

In order for the United States to maintain a strong, responsible democracy with a prosperous economy, much more will be required than the enunciation of national goals. Both federal and state initiatives must support the right mix of educational vision, standards of performance, and investment in technology. These strategies must be linked to a willingness on the part of educators to respond to a changing world by changing the schools.

The new reform strategy must be comprehensive and spring from an understanding of what needs to be learned and how to teach it. The type of curriculum and instruction used must be sophisticated with a viable academic base.

And above all, the focus on school improvement must center on the elementary schools with special attention to teaching and learning in grades K-3. Past educational policy and practice has failed to call for and demand specified student outcomes in the primary grades. The wave of future reform considers this action the first order of business.

CHARTER SCHOOLS

Inherent in President Bush's plans for education reform is the exciting concept that any organization meeting minimum state criteria could be chartered as a public school and granted the right to accept students and receive public money.

Education Alternatives Inc., a private, for-profit firm from Minneapolis, has already developed a national model for chartering public schools and opened the first privately operated public school in America in the fall of 1991. The firm contracted with the Dade County, Florida, School Board to manage a new elementary school in an urban setting. The Miami school is located in a depressed area where about 95 percent of the population qualify for public assistance.

The firm currently operates two private schools, called Tesseract schools, one in Paradise Valley, Arizona, the other in Eagan, Minnesota. As the corporation moves into the area of chartering and operating public schools, the curriculum and methods developed in these two private schools will be duplicated in the public schools which it operates for profit.

John Golle, chairman of the Board of Education Alternatives, contends that he can operate a first class private or public school at a cost of $5,000.00 per pupil. This is considerably less expensive than the average per pupil cost for the nation's public schools, currently estimated by the U.S. Department of Education to be $5,638 per year.

Tesseract schools operate on the premise that at least one third of a child's academic achievement occurs before first grade, and there is an 85 percent correlation between school achievement in the third grade and school achievement in the eleventh grade.

The Tesseract school program places priority on fundamental skills that will give children a foundation for the future. Curriculum concentration is on reading, writing, math, science, foreign languages, and computer literacy. The curriculum also includes music, art, and physical education. Personal attention and advanced technology are combined to give children the best of what modern education has to offer. Large group, small group, and individual learning formats are used as the delivery system. Children are stimulated to perform above grade level as measured by standardized state and national tests.

Under the Tesseract model, individual learning abilities, interests, and learning styles play an important role in how well a child learns. The curriculum is customized for each student. At the start of the school year, parents, teachers, and each child sit down to develop a Personal Education Plan (PEP). It includes the goals the child will be challenged to achieve and the resources, teachers, time, and materials needed for success.

The objective is to lay a foundation early that will help children throughout the "formal" learning years. Tesseract aims at developing well-rounded, self-confident individuals, who possess superior academic skills and enjoy learning.

Teachers in Tesseract schools believe, as do many researchers, that 80 percent of all learners can achieve at the same level as the top 20 percent if instruction is tailored to their individual rates and styles.

The eyes of the education world will certainly be on South Pointe elementary school in Miami Beach for the next several years. The marketing arrangement is not just bold and innovative, it is a radical departure from the business community's tradition of offering education advice but not actively participating in finding better solutions. Not the least of the up-coming experiment is academic performance regardless of students' educational or economic background.

To achieve the desired student-teacher ratio of one to twelve, the school will employ first-year graduate students as part-time teachers. The aides will be paid $7.00 an hour and get credits towards a master's degree in education.

The implications of a burgeoning reform in which private firms can manage public schools for profit will most definitely have a profound effect upon the way public schools now operate. With alternatives to government operated schools waiting in the wings, public school administrators had better begin scrambling to get their act together. Under the plan of choice, only the details need working out for private education to move from bit player to center stage in the nation's school reform movement.

In mid 1991 Chris Whittle, the media innovator who launched the "Channel One" television news program now in use in schools, announced plans to develop a nationwide chain of for-profit schools which are designed from the ground up. The initial $60 million planned for research will come from Whittle Communications, which is half-owned by Time Warner, Inc. and one-third from a British newspaper publishing company.

The proposed "Whittle Schools" plan to achieve the goal of underpricing local public schools by harnessing student power to reduce support staff and bureaucracy. Extensive peer teaching is an idea being considered. The schools will serve all students including the handicapped and others with special needs from birth to age eighteen.

In making the announcement, Mr. Whittle stressed that while the proposed schools will be oriented towards profit making, they will have a larger public purpose to demonstrate a new brand of education, unburdened by multiple layers of educational bureaucracy which are unwilling to change from the status quo.

The planned research has been named the "Edison Project," a reference to the revolutionary shift from candle power to the light bulb. The new firm is receptive to offers to manage individual public schools as well as entire school systems.

At present no other major corporations are planning to operate for-profit schools on the scale proposed by Whittle communications. The scope of the project is two hundred schools in major areas by 1996 at a cost of $2.5 billion to $3 billion. By the year 2010 the firm expects to be serving up to two million pupils on one thousand school campuses.

HONDA'S SCHOOL PLAN

Corporate officials of the American Honda Corporation have launched one of the largest corporate efforts to support American education to date. Honda is making plans to invest $25 million in a mission to develop experimental boarding schools for at-risk students. The plan is to develop models which can be replicated by other communities.

STATE CHARTERED SCHOOLS ACTION

Minnesota is leading the states in the movement to establish "charter" or outcome based schools. Legislation has been passed authorizing school boards to establish a limited number of chartered schools. The schools, which are "exempt from all statutes and rules applicable to a school board or school district," can be limited to one grade or focused on certain subjects such as the fine arts, mathematics, science or a foreign language. (Minnesota School Law, 1990)

Expansion of charter schools is certain to be one of the waves of the future. Once the notion of choice is applied to private schools, an increase in the number of chartered schools can be expected to accelerate.

CHAPTER 2

Demography of the Elementary Schools in the 1990's

The number of children of elementary school age reached its highest point (36.7 million) in 1970. This figure dropped to thirty million by 1983 and is expected to peak at 34.4 million in 1995. Then, the number will start falling again and fluctuate between thirty-two and thirty-four million during most of the 21st century.

As the nation prepares for a new influx of elementary school children, the changing demography of the schools' population, coupled with changing family lifestyles, calls for restyled elementary schools.

Up to now, entirely too little attention has been paid to how population shifts in the United States are recasting the mission of the nation's elementary schools. The number of elementary school age children is once again on the rise, and this time a disproportionate collection of them are nonwhite, poor, and from single parent homes. The elementary school population epitomizes the trend of the nation, which is increasingly growing less white.

Furthermore, traditions associated with the two-parent family, the church, and small town life are on the wane. To take up the slack, schools are being asked to guide the national culture almost singlehandedly through a storm of change, while assimilating the most diverse and challenging student population in American history.

Although the nation has become more ethnically heterogenous, schools have failed to well educate either minorities or women. For example, more women than men participated in the 1990 Scholastic Aptitude Test, yet the women scored lower than men on both the verbal and mathematics sections. This disgraceful discrepancy is the direct fault of elementary and secondary schooling, since there is no difference in native intelligence between the sexes.

An outcome of changing family lifestyles is that children born in the past twenty years are experiencing family environments unknown to children of any other generation:

Census Bureau data on this phenomenon is as follows:

- 26 percent of children born in 1987 were to unmarried mothers.
- 20 percent live with a mother with no father present in the home.
- 45 percent of all children live in homes where both parents work.

The racial demography of children approaching school age is even more dramatic and reflects socioeconomic conditions different from any we have known in the past.

- 50 percent of the black children reside only with their mother.
- 70 percent of the above mentioned children live in poverty.
- 60 percent of the black children born in 1985 were born out of wedlock.
- 50 percent of the above mentioned children were born to a teenager.
- 51 percent of black mothers have never married.
  (National Center for Health Statistics Vol. 39 #4 1988)

What all this means is that the composition of schools is becoming increasingly diverse in race, color, socioeconomic characteristics, and family background.

In 1870 when the government first started keeping records, blacks made up 19.3 percent of the total U.S. population. This number decreased steadily to 9.7 percent by 1930, but since then it has been slowly rising. Blacks are at 12.1 percent of the population and are expected to reach 14.4 percent in 2010.

As birth rates of Americans other than whites increase, the schools must embrace a more enlightened notion of equality and inclusion. The effort to improve education cannot be sustained on the basis of policies which exile large populations of minorities to the margins of society.

Another challenge for schools is the ever increasing number of children born, often prematurely, to teenage mothers. Because of their low birth weight and underdeveloped immune system, these children are vulnerable to an array of diseases which can impede physical and cognitive development. This problem is compounded by the fact that teenage mothers often live in poverty, which engenders other risk factors such as poor prenatal care, malnutrition, domestic violence, and drug abuse.

How many such children are headed for our schools? Of the 3.3 million births a year in the United States, 700,000 babies are almost assured of being educationally retarded or "difficult to teach" due to complications associated with premature birth. The schools can alter these conditions by confronting them head on.

The new demographics of the school population require that elementary schools develop a capacity to support and sustain the family in its task of raising children. This is a role not previously encountered, and its initiation calls for a new sensitivity towards minority and disadvantaged children.

Minority youngsters already are, or soon will be, in the majority in the public schools of some states. An example of the diversity confronting schools is the language minority-majority phenomenon. The nation's twenty-five largest city school systems now have a majority of language minority students, and while the population of the United States is predicted to grow only marginally in the next decade (from 246 million to 265 million), the rate of minority growth is so fast that by 2001 approximately 91 million of the population will be minorities, predominantly of school age.

The U.S. Department of Education projects that the number of children between the ages of five and fourteen who are limited in their English proficiency will have increased by a staggering 42 percent in the last decade of this century. Therefore, elementary schools must be prepared to contend with a widening range of instructional and curricular implications associated with language minority students.

The percentage of non-English-speaking children entering school is much greater in some states than others. For example, about 25 percent of California entering students have limited ability to speak, comprehend, or write English. In all grades and all states, limited English-speaking students must receive language support until they attain proficiency.

Schools can no longer operate in a vacuum, ignoring the demography of their population. There have been tremendous structural changes in the American family, but schools still function as if they are serving families with the lifestyle of a father working and a mother at home. In a changing society, schools must alter their mission to engage the challenges wrought by new family lifestyles.

Beginning immediately, all schools should collect data on the numbers of children from single parent families as well as families where both parents are employed outside the home. This data is essential in order to plan school programs to meet the changing needs of families in transition.

School boards must recognize America's demographic shift to single parent, teenage parent, and two wage earner families and must realize what those trends mean to education. Coping with this issue calls for reorganizing and extending the school day to accommodate children who have no one at home at the end of the conventional school day.

Furthermore, schools must begin monitoring the progress of black and Hispanic students. In the past, schools, particularly urban schools, have scrupulously avoided collecting data by race, fearing the data would underscore gaps between white and minority achievement. This oversight has been an attempt to avoid provoking controversy. But if the gaps are to be closed, achievement differences must be examined and worked on.

Schools know that the data they collect on achievement is going to be unfavorable to blacks and Hispanics, but by failing to examine differences in student performance as it relates to race and ethnicity, they fail to understand the action needed to narrow the gap. By not having information on where the students are in the learning process, school staffs are unable to address the equity issue, which urgently needs attention.

Previously reported data notes that the college-going rate for Hispanics and blacks has declined for the last ten years. At the same time, black enlistment in the armed forces increased in the 1980's. The problem is, there exists no performance data on race and ethnic groups in elementary schools and this is where deficiencies must be remedied.

Urban schools attempt to justify their failure to collect data about the performance of minority students with the excuse that they want to be "race neutral." Following desegregation action, they have aspired towards being "color blind" with the result that they have failed to monitor and assess action which needs to be taken to support greater learning by race and ethnic groups.

America's school reform efforts should diagram schools around the demography of the students to be served in a particular community. Schooling should be crafted to accommodate the numbers of children coming from homes in which both parents are in the work force, the percentage of children from single parent homes, and the ethnic and racial makeup of the community.

School reform efforts must also give special consideration to the family lifestyles of disadvantaged children being served by a particular school. This means that schools, when dealing with children on the margin of society, must pick up and teach the "hidden curriculum" which family life has imparted to children in the past. Central to the idea of school reform is the concept of making the school more responsive to changing family lifestyles.

Changing demographics and the growing diversity of the student population are forcing elementary schools to search for school practices which will accommodate diversity without loss of equality. If the nation is to maintain an internationally competitive science community and economy, the schools must respond to the challenges of an array of converging demographic and educational trends.

THE AT-RISK SYNDROME

The elementary school is the key arena for coping with children who are commonly referred to as being at-risk. Edward Zigler, one of the founders of Head Start, constructed the following model as a quick way of identifying at-risk children:

- the economically disadvantaged
- those with limited English proficiency
- the handicapped

The nation's expanding demography has enlarged this model to include children with the following difficulties:

- divorced parents
- latchkey children
- substance abuse
- premature birth
- poverty
- teenage parent
- single female parent
- neglected children
- Native American parents
- incarcerated parents
- incarcerated siblings
  (*Head Start: The Nation's Pride* 4/18/90)

Children in any one of the above categories may be at risk; children falling into two or more definitely are.

In past years the gathering of social data about children was frowned upon as being an invasion of privacy. Recent research reflects that if schools are to successfully control the nation's dropout syndrome, which is now at 30 percent, then they must both gather social data and implement educational intervention hinged upon the available information. Programs, curricula, and activities must be designed to minimize the dropout risk based upon the demography of the children served by a particular school.

With prison data reflecting that 85.5 percent of prison inmates are dropouts, it is essential that society take advantage of the elementary school setting as the place to intervene and help everyone succeed in school.

In view of demographic projections that by the year 2000, one-third of the U.S. workforce will include adults who are now children at-risk, school years K-3 must be more focused to better educate this group of children. In the effort to accomplish this task, policies and programs should not concentrate just on the child but should simultaneously address the parent, as the two are interdependent. Responsive parents are a vital connection in educating at-risk children, and all elementary schools should implement family support initiatives.

As the nation approaches the end of the twentieth century, many studies of education have identified serious problems caused by the changing demographics of both the states and the nation's population. The studies are unanimous in their conclusion that our schools are ill-preparing children of European descent for the twenty-first century. They also are in agreement that minority groups including African American, Latin American, and Native Americans are particularly ill-served. By every quantifiable measure large numbers of minority children are achieving poorly.

When the low achievement of minority children is linked to demgoraphics showing that the numbers and percentage of these children are rapidly increasing, the issue becomes critical. Reform strategies to better educate all children but especially minorities are vital if public education is to survive.

Demographic trends point to serious shortfalls of mathematically prepared workers. At all grade levels relatively few blacks or Hispanics excel in mathematics. Elementary schools need to initiate action to turn this situation around. Unless this critical education deficit is addressed with expedience, the nation's need for a scientifically oriented workforce will not be met.

We are already experiencing a shortfall in scientific workers, to which Congress has surprisingly responded by raising immigration quotas for immigrants able to do scientific and technical labor. Many educational observers view this action with alarm, fearing that it will divert attention from the growing gulf in the education of minorities versus non-minorities.

The children of poverty, who are largely minorities, already make up a disproportionate percentage of the at-risk children. This group, more than any other, is educationally neglected. By all measures their achievement in school is far below that of middle class white children. If the present disparity in achievement is allowed to continue, the nation will find itself with a permanent underclass of unemployed at the same time that technology creates whole new categories of jobs to go begging. Unless the endangered children receive a better education in the elementary schools, then we are headed for a soup kitchen labor force. Intense pressure should be put on elementary schools to make them more responsive to the needs of blacks and Hispanics, not just for the sake of the nation but in the interest of the children.

What is coming toward the education system is a group of children who will be poorer, more ethnically and linguistically diverse, and with more handicaps. These children will be both more difficult and more expensive to teach.

CHAPTER 3

Elementary Education In The 1990's

"THE RELENTLESS PURSUIT OF EXCELLENCE"

America cannot prosper unless its schools are successful. Therein lies the problem. The purpose of education is unchanged, but the world has changed and the schools are having difficulty adapting.

The education enterprise is so massive and so complicated that national and state governments have had limited influence. Meaningful education reform must be initiated at the local level where the needs of individual students and communities are best known. Yet school boards, superintendents, and principals who administer local schools are renowned for their timidity and diffidence when it comes to innovation and change in school curricula, instruction, and mode of operation.

The outcome of this pusillanimity is a major erosion of confidence in both the existing system of schooling and in educators for their failure to produce desirable learning outcomes in children attending schools under their control. Disillusionment with bureaucratization and standardization of educational practice has reached the boiling point.

Study after study has documented the poor performance of elementary school students in every subject area in comparison with those of other countries, but our most perilous folly is an absolute inability to educate poor and minority children.

New programs of the highest priority need to be targeted to improving achievement for those children.

The educational dilemma becomes even more perplexing when we face the issue that, the nation's school system must anticipate a group of children with more handicaps which will surely affect the nature of their schooling. A nation in jeopardy cannot afford to ignore its children at-risk, with their syndromes of failure in school, early school leaving, pregnancy, and drug abuse. The socioeconomic implications of this influx are enormous.

Nearly one half of the nation's children are now growing up in families which are not viable from an educational standpoint. Many parents come home from work exhausted, both physically and mentally. Frequent divorces and a bewildering array of relationships have left many homes with a serious parenting deficit.

The absence of a stable home environment with close loving supervision has not been properly corrected by child care facilities where babysitters often do little more than ensure that children stay out of harm's way. The outcome is that children are coming to school with no self-discipline and without having acquired the personality traits essential to study skills in reading and mathematics.

The sorry state of education for minority children compels a major reexamination by the school districts across the nation of their elementary schools. Root causes for the absence of quality and success in the education of minority children must be pinpointed and corrected. With a sense of urgency, school districts should address better ways of educating all children, but especially the poor and minority groups. A first order of the day is for educators to raise their expectations for these children; they can no longer afford to neglect a significant portion of the rising generation.

Elementary schools have failed to come to grips with even the most basic issue involving minorities. As a group, black males are greatly overrepresented among the under educated, the jobless, the jailed, and the unmarried. Effectively preparing children (black males and others) should be a major priority for the elementary schools. Otherwise, the number of alienated and malfunctioning adults will further bifurcate the nation's social structure in the coming decades.

The elementary schools must target children from low income families and perform effective intervention, providing both nurturing and the instruction that they need in order to prepare themselves for a difficult future.

The most significant challenge, then, is to educate well students from minority cultures and low income families; in other words, make the schools work for people who need education most. We are rapidly becoming a nation of minorities and the challenge is to improve education for the least privileged as well as the most fortunate.

In addition to the minority problem, a whole litany of other social issues is crippling the schools, including the breakup of the family, poverty, drugs, and the way the schools treat parents as unimportant influences on children.

It is imperative that American education for the first time become concerned about the quality of education for all students, not excusing some students from achieving on the basis of their race, gender, or disabilities. Heading the reform agenda, then, is the issue of improving outcomes for all students.

One approach is to establish "superior" schools. These are schools which have accepted the responsibility to educate and succeed with all children, and they do whatever is necessary to make that happen. Their mission is to "unteach" the teaching staff of the notion that they cannot teach some children. Researchers tell us that we are not educating 25 to 30 percent of the elementary school population who do not do well in school. This is a luxury we can no longer afford.

Lagging achievement of poor children is one of the chief reasons for reform. Raising standards without developing new strategies for reaching these children will only push them further behind. A major challenge is to successfully devise learning environments that promote success for children who are currently failing.

Perhaps the first thing schools must do is to get over the notion that children's education and development is a six-hour-a-day phenomenon that happens only at school. They must recognize that education is determined to a considerable extent by home life. Schools have for too long attempted to compartmentalize children and failed to regard them as family members or members of society. Until this attitude changes, not much is going to happen.

As the numbers of minority children continue to increase, the population in schools becomes increasingly diverse. In large numbers of schools, more than 50 percent of the children can qualify for categorical programs. These are special programs for children with problems in which funding is earmarked and cannot be spent for anything else.

Increasing numbers of children are coming to school poorly equipped to begin learning. They may be victims of teenage pregnancy or an environment of drugs and alcohol. The implication here is that the learning environment must be made more dynamic to cope with children who are difficult to teach.

First, there must be a reassertion of what children need to learn, and an agreement that some things are more worth learning than others. Children must be prepared for a worldwide marketplace. There must be a strong emphasis on languages other than English and an understanding of other countries. And perhaps, most important of all, the schools' new curricula must be accompanied by a deepening interest in the study of citizen responsibility in a democratic government.

What is required is more action at the district level as school districts begin to distinguish themselves in academic improvement. Otherwise, we will end up like third world countries, at the bottom of the educational heap. The difference between districts will continue to widen as some districts do things which are really special.

In brief, public concern about education is beginning to focus on the failure of public schools to adequately educate minority students who now constitute more than half of the student enrollment in some states. Small improvements are no longer acceptable. Education must begin to operate at a new plateau of student performance, teacher productivity, and cost effectiveness.

Hard experience reflects that we simply are not getting our money's worth in education. Our focus must no longer be on resources. It must zero in on results. This means that schools must experiment with finding new ways for doing things. Of course some of the experiments will not work out, but experimentation is preferable to the status quo because the status quo could hardly be worse.

GRADE RETENTION: A REPRESSIVE EDUCATIONAL PRACTICE

After a ten-year trend of increasingly stricter policies requiring low achievement students to repeat a grade, many educational leaders are beginning to question this practice and assess alternative approaches to dealing with the problem.

The increase in formal retention policies during the 1980's is due, at least in part, to the educational excellence movement and its call for higher standards. Repeating a grade has long been considered an acceptable way of bringing children up to standard. The educational practice of forcing academically troubled students to repeat a grade reflects an assumption on the part of educators that they will mature, master deficient skills, and be less likely to fail again. In reality, grade retention is a stifling measure which has long been a naive response to the complex problem of educating low achievers.

An educational policy which forces students to spend a second year on the same material is a crude and primitive strategy for individualizing instruction. Common sense tells us that school districts have an obligation to provide detained students with different instruction the second time around, but the evidence is clear that this is not what has been going on.

Data on the amount of retention in many districts is not available, but the statistics are appalling from the districts which do keep records. Equally disturbing is data which reflects that students retained consist of a disproportionate percentage of boys, minorities, and children from low income families.

In 1989 the Cleveland school district failed to promote 14 percent of its 72,000 students (*Education Week* 5/16/90). In an attempt to cover up increasing high retention rates, a district superintendent announced a lowering of standards for promoting students. It is impossible to understand why school districts spend so much time tinkering with standards instead of targeting children for special assistance. They consistently miss the point that student outcomes are the only measure of a school's success.

Among large urban school districts, one of the worst retention rates is in the Philadelphia school district, which retains 22 percent of its students in grades one to eight each year (*Education Week* 5/16/90). Justification for retention is a combination of teacher judgment and test scores. Furthermore, Philadelphia, like many other school districts, is plagued with multiple retention (students retained more than once).

While Philadelphia's retention figure is one of the highest among individual school districts, Florida leads the states in the numbers of students required to repeat a grade. Up to one third of all Florida students are now retained by the time they reach the fourth grade. In the 1987–88 school year Florida school districts retained more than 17,000 children in kindergarten. The 1988 cost to the state for remediating 12 percent of all kindergarteners amounted to $43.5 million. Thirteen thousand children repeated the first grade at a cost of $35.1 million.

Because a void in leadership at the local level has failed to deal with the problem of grade retention, Florida legislators, along with law makers in a number of other states, are initiating legislation eliminating grades K through 3 and requiring educators to come up with viable multi-grading plans. Wide ranging school reform legislation in many states is projected to replace grades K-3 with a primary school program in which children progress at their own pace in multi-age groupings. In this setting, the first years of education, kindergarten through grade three, are reorganized into a single unit and the rigid grade levels are blurred. The motivation behind those reforms is extensive research showing that (1) retention does not help students and (2) it is a major contributing factor to the rising dropout rate.

Like Florida, Massachusetts is a state attempting to do something about the repressive practice of grade retention. Massachusetts school districts retained 28,233 students in the 1989–90 school year at an average per pupil cost of $4,259 and a state wide cost of $120 million.

Harold Raynolds Jr., commissioner of education, has

urged all Massachusetts school districts to cease retaining low achieving students in a grade. In calling for new strategies to cope with the retention problem, Commissioner Raynolds charged, "Public schools are significantly increasing school budgets by retaining students without any indication that the money is well spent" (Mass. State Board of Education Minutes April 1990).

While there is no reliable national data on the number of public school students retained in a grade each year, Larrie A. Shepard, co-editor of a 1989 book on the subject, estimates that 2.4 million students are retained annually at a cost of $10 billion for the extra year of schooling.

Meanwhile, many school systems across the nation engage in the practice of "social promotion." This is the process of promoting youngsters who are not up to standard, but paying no further attention to their lack of skills. Schools involved in this practice should begin talking about normal grade promotion with a plus factor. This means not simply socially promoting students, but following through with continuing assistance and support.

THE EFFECTS OF RETENTION

Researchers studying the effects of retention are unanimous that the practice is repressive and subjects students to embarrassment, humiliation, and loss of self-concept. Those who are held back (1) learn less the following years, (2) develop negative self-concepts, (3) are more likely to drop out of school, (4) are more likely to get into trouble with the law.

The outcomes for individual students who have been detained are (1) lowered levels of achievement and self-esteem, (2) increased dependence on society for support, (3) a sense of frustration and defeat. Schools should cease retaining students, when doing so will only force them to repeat the same grade in the same way. Retention in one grade increases the likelihood of dropping out to 50 percent. Retention in two grades increases the likelihood to 90 percent.

The movement away from rigid retention policies is strongest in the early grades. The social and academic development of youngsters at this age is very rapid and uneven. Certainly it is inappropriate to retain children between kindergarten and grade three.

Some states' lawmakers have grown impatient with children who have not learned by the time they reach the third grade and require children to pass a test before moving into the fourth grade. Lawmakers rightfully, because of their role in funding education, feel that at some point children must attain certain basic competencies.

But sometimes they go too far. Georgia legislators assumed that when children did poorly on a first grade test, they would be bettor off if they repeated kindergarten. Subsequently, legislation was passed mandating retention for all who failed the test. Had the legislators examined the evidence, they would have found a dozen controlled research studies showing no benefit to achievement from an extra year program before first grade. The research also connotes that retention has very negative effects on children's attitudes and self-esteem.

Georgia is only one of many states which mistakenly believe that retention in the early grades is an effective measure. As mentioned earlier, Florida's schools (1987–1988) retained 17,000 kindergarteners. The retention track record is equally exorbitant in a number of other states. Data is clear that kindergarten retention does not improve achievement in first grade or in the years following first grade.

Retention clearly consigns children to ineffective and stigmatizing treatment with no evidence of increased learning. The children who are retained are the same ones whose lives are already haunted by failure and insecurity in realms outside the school.

Evidence that many school districts have turned their backs on the retention problem is seen in the fact that in some elementary schools in a particular district there are few or no retentions in the kindergarten and first grade. Yet other schools nearby continue to detain large numbers of students. There is simply no explanation as to why retention is nonexistent in some schools and runs as high as 20 percent in other schools in the same district.

Two aspects of the retention practice are clear: (1) blanket retention policies are not in the best interest of children; (2)

educators have failed miserably to come up with viable alternatives.

Dismaying data on grade retention research indicates that teachers are often pressured by their colleagues to retain students. Frequently, teachers in a higher grade embarrass and humiliate teachers in a lower grade by sending promoted students back to them.

Retention rates make it clear that there are large numbers of students who are not prepared to move on to the next grade, and yet educators have failed to develop a better system.

But the financial cost of retention is very high. However, it is hidden in a school system's general education budget and billed to the state in the form of per pupil cost. The healthy thing about the debate over retention is that it pinpoints deficiencies in practice and the lack of quality in education offered to many students.

Schools have the responsibility for making sure that all children learn. Instead of retaining large numbers of students, districts should develop alternative policies to ensure that all students succeed. Reform policies must include (1) changes in curricula, (2) new methods of grouping students, (3) the use of mentors in a support system.

A SYSTEM OF UNINTERRUPTED LEARNING

With all of the pressure applied to improving schools over the last few years it is incomprehensible that administrators have made no effort to change the system and find a better model. The shameful levels of performance of students in conventional elementary schools cry out for forceful action, but little administrative initiative has been forthcoming. Yet, it is increasingly apparent that the way schools are currently organized is not working for many children.

A major drawback to schools, as they are now constituted, is their failure to recognize and cope with wide diversity in students' learning and the increasing gap in students' skills as they move through the system. While it seems inconceivable, most of the nation's elementary schools continue to use lock-step approaches to learning regardless of individual student differences and needs. Coping with diversity and organizing the system into a more effective learning environment are the major challenges confronting the nation's elementary schools' staffs.

As currently structured, elementary schools are fairly successful places for children with above average academic ability. But those with average or below average skills find them to be unappealing places, without reality, where little or no attention is paid to their needs.

Schools have always had two alternatives for students who have difficulty in learning: change the students or change the schools. The schools have always won out. The universally accepted practice is to change the students with scant regard for the consequences. The outcome becomes one of disciplining and punishing recalcitrant students who do not adjust easily to the establishment's ironclad programs.

An analogy to the schools' philosophy on this issue is to compare their practice to that of Procrustes, the legendary robber of ancient Greece. The fabled Procrustes tied his victims to an iron bed and if they did not fit, he either stretched their legs, or chopped them off to make them conform to the length of the bed.

Assuming an unfeeling Procrustean-like posture, schools' staffs stretch or restrain the intellect of their clients to fit the instruction of the grade. As a consequence, schools alienate and discard recalcitrant students who do not adapt to the established lockstep system.

The conformity of conventional elementary schools is a failed strategy, graphically illustrated by the nation's present functional illiteracy rate of 40 percent along with a 30 percent dropout rate. Data such as these are no longer defensible.

A more logical solution to the lack of fit between students and schools is to change the schools. Instead of grouping students by age, a challenging alternative is to group them by achievement. The intent is to attain the right balance by adjusting the subject matter to fit the student's ability and learning style and placing learning on a continuum.

The reform most likely to radically change primary education (K-3) goes by a number of names, but there is only one objective: to make learning more developmentally appropriate.

The most often used terms describing the early stirrings of this trend are cross age groupings, multi-grade settings, multi-age grouping, mixed age grouping, nongraded classes, and continuous progress.

The operative principle is that children's development, as often as not, does not match their grade level and they will learn more efficiently when more appropriately placed and allowed to develop at their own pace.

In a system of continuous progress, tasks proceed in a logical cumulative sequence without repetition. Each task is designed to have meaning and significance to the students. Tasks vary, with some assignments being completed by individuals, while others are accomplished in pairs or small groups of from three to five students. An objective of educational reform is more active participation in learning by the students and less domination though the lecture method by teachers.

The system for grouping children on the basis of stages of development and achievement instead of age, is perhaps most appropriately referred to as continuous progress. This type of organization is highly effective in coping with the range of academic diversity found in groups of children, especially children in the public schools.

While this innovation in elementary school organization has been around for a long time, only a few avant-garde schools have experimented with implementation. The vast majority of schools continue to struggle with the conventional system of grouping children by age into grades.

The failure of elementary education to achieve substantively higher outcomes in learning can be largely attributed to a lack of attention to the diversity among children assigned to a particular grade. Here, the span in both achievement and development is enormous.

In traditional graded schools, students who fall behind do not make up lost ground but continue to drop further behind over time. After a while the discrepancy in learning widens to the point where slower students are making little or no progress. Their lack of learning places them at risk to leave school early, partly because they are falling further behind and receiving little or no academic assistance or social support for improvement and partly because they are often truant for an inordinate amount of time. School alienation has long been known to be the major reason for truancy. Too often remedial instruction to help students keep up is not available, or if offered, is not socially acceptable.

The continuous progress system is based upon flexible grouping and tracking policies. Further, it includes a strategy for pinpointing students who need extra help and those with poor academic status so their instruction can be varied to apply to their particular learning style. Special assistance should always be available for children who need extra help with a learning task; this help can come in the form of volunteers, peer tutors, and aides. However, some children simply require more time. Learning strategies available in a continuous progress system for students who need more time and special assistance in mastering the skills needed for the next level of learning are longer day programs, Saturday attendance, and summer continuation schools. Students who fall behind should be engaged in one or more of these activities.

Teachers have always established special conditions in the learning environment for some students (especially bright students). These conditions are equally important for all students (especially slower students).

It is no more odd for students to need extra time to finish elementary school than it is for students to take six or seven years to complete graduate school. There is nothing strange about the fact that some students need several weeks to understand fractions while others can work with them competently after three or four lessons.

A bright child, trapped in the unchallenging environment of school routine as practiced in graded schools, becomes a child at-risk. While adults are uncomfortable in boring situations, young children of primary age find boredom frustrating and unbearable.

Too many schools fail to provide special instruction for gifted children on the grounds that special programs planned for bright children are elitist. Yet these same school officials who assume this posture will provide special athletic competition for talented athletes to the exclusion of others and not consider this action elitist.

A system of continuous progress allows forward movement for the gifted as well as making special provisions for more awkward learners who need time and individual attention. The goal is for every child by grade three to read with understanding, compute with accuracy, and speak and listen effectively.

What are educators doing about the widening diversity in learning among students? In conventional graded schools, the usual approach is to reduce the span of disparity. Unfortunately, the dimensions of difference are usually reduced by limiting the advancement of capable students. This narrow approach to academic diversity is no longer acceptable. All students should learn at their best pace and no effort should be made to lessen the variances in learning. Grouping patterns for students should be flexible and subject to change as student learning increases.

Students vary widely in the speed of their learning, and those whose pace is awkward or slow must be deliberately targeted to receive special assistance. Properly implemented, the continuous progress model has a special component to employ a variety of remediation strategies for students who are behind or having difficulty learning. These strategies include both academic assistance and social support. They target students who require more time, different methods, more essentials, and extra encouragement in order to learn. These resources are then engaged.

The first task in multi-age grouping is to target problem learners with levels of instruction and materials appropriate to the academic work at hand. Their progress is accelerated by the use of social support systems which encourage active rather than passive learning. Social support techniques include (1) high participation in class (2) recognizing student improvement (3) opportunities for student interaction in groups.

Underlying the opportunities for students to reach set standards is a system which will allow ample time for them to complete the task at hand. Blurring grade lines and concentrating on individual achievement will give teachers the flexibility needed to accomplish this goal.

A challenging supportive environment for clumsy and erratic learners should focus first and foremost on the acquisition of strong reading skills. Reading is the most important subject in the elementary school, and all other activities can be suspended or delayed until students begin to master this subject.

Most objections to a system deploying students out of the grade into a more flexible arrangement come from administrators who argue that children should be kept together by age. The fallacy of this argument is quickly disproved by a simple survey of the ages of the children within the various grades of the school. One such survey recently found that by the time children reached the third grade, there was as much as a five year age spread between the youngest and oldest child.

Research reports that by the fourth grade, test scores reveal that six full grades separate children in the top and bottom reading groups. When math is measured, four full grades separate those in the top and bottom groups (Goodlad) 1984).

The first initiative in multi-aging in elementary schools should begin with primary age children. Once the principal and staff feel comfortable with a routine where the younger children are deployed on the basis of learning skills rather than grade levels, then the system can be applied to intermediate age children.

When a school moves to the ungraded model, changes are made in the way learning is delivered. Teachers cease the routine of making sterotyped inquiry into material for which they have pat answers. The image of the teacher shifts from one of conveyor of knowledge to a remover of roadblocks. Actually this idea of the role of teacher is not new. This was envisioned in the dialogues of Socrates who compared the function of the teacher to that of the midwife. The teacher should deliver learning, not dispense knowledge. In this setting much of the burden of learning shifts from the teacher to the student.

Simple recall spurred by rudimentary questions is the lowest order of intellectual activity. More rigorous intellectual activities going up the scale are comprehension, application, analysis, synthesis, and evaluation.

While the use of simple questions by teachers has learning value, teachers must spend more time in preparing sophisticated questions which pose enigmas. This means that classroom activity moves from a feedback of facts towards problem solving activity. The elementary classroom becomes a laboratory of learning with a mix of children of different ages learning at varying pace.

With school reform efforts focusing more and more on the importance of the early years, Vito Perrone, director of teacher education programs at Harvard, notes a growing recognition of the "need to provide children with a very strong base, out of which they can move confidently into the upper grades" Perrone suggests that the primary years should be considered as "a developmental period where some children will move more rapidly than others" (Conversation with the Author, 1987). Dr. Perrone's observations are reinforced by virtually all of the policy reports on primary age children, which support the ungraded model as the most effective system for dealing with individual differences among children of that age.

The chief obstacle to embracing ungraded primaries as a more competent arrangement for teaching younger children is the argument of elementary principals that placing children in grades is a more efficient way to manage large numbers of children. No one questions the efficiency of the grade as a device for controlling children, but when the learning outcomes of children are considered rather than the convenience of administrators, the ungraded approach has distinct advantages.

Multi-age grouping accommodates a wide variation in children's rates of learning while eliminating the evils of social promotion and grade retention. Further, in recognizing wide patterns of learning, it does away with stigmatizing many children as slow learners, a label now being given to 40 percent of all children. Other gains include improved chances of good mental health and a positive attitude towards schools. Policy reports suggest that multi-graded classrooms are particularly beneficial for boys, underachievers, minorities, and low income students.

Many educators who have not carefully examined continuous progress learning in depth, incorrectly perceive that the ungraded model is without structure, a situation where students are turned loose to do their own thing. This is a misconception of profound proportions. A good ungraded model operates on a highly articulated structure which undergirds and supports individual learning.

The vast expenditures of the Charles F. Kettering Foundation in the seventies and the colossal failure of its program of Individually Guided Education, a program designed to individualize learning within the grade, conclusively prove that we cannot achieve an effective individualized curriculum within graded classes. Policy makers in a number of states recognized this phenomenon and legislated non-graded primaries in their 1990 legislative sessions.

The major obstacle to be overcome by a school contemplating a move from age grouping to multi-age grouping is how to untrain teachers who have been taught to think in terms of distinct grade structures and are unprepared for a major curriculum structural change. This is a significant problem, as the most critical variable in dealing with differences in developmental stages and wide variations in learning is the ability of the teacher. For example, ungraded methods require that teachers have more detailed knowledge about each student's development and learning style. Continuous progress demands more administrative support and a higher quality of school leadership than it takes to head a conventional graded school. The undertaking is not more costly, but adjustments need to be made to give the teachers more time for planning.

The challenge of the multi-age model of schooling is to offer a more sophisticated curriculum to support mixed age learning. The present state of curricula in elementary schools is relatively unsophisticated. In multi-age classes, schools are prepared to cope with a much greater diversity of learning than currently exists in the grade level model. Some primary age children will be doing work comparable to the present sixth grade while others will need five or six years to become highly proficient in, what is now taught in grades K-3.

By grouping children more flexibly and targeting instruction to meet a wider range of abilities in the classroom, the practice of multi-aging offers a higher quality of education for all of its clientele. Among welcome changes, the ungraded primary eliminates "Pull outs" for remedial and special education students. A major complaint of classroom teachers is that children who are pulled out of class for special instruction miss material which the teacher must later repeat for their benefit.

In summary, schools should organize across-age learning

around developmental stages rather than grades. Learning will then take place on a continuum in early childhood, middle childhood, and early adolescence.

TEACHING IN TEAMS

Inherent in the practice of breaking out of the age-grade pattern of grouping is the reorganization of the teaching staff into teams. This mode of teaching allows schools to reduce significantly the ratio of adults to children and consequently give children the attention they require.

In the typical elementary school classroom, teachers manage a large group of students and are isolated much of the day from one another in their respective classrooms.

In this type of situation, teaching is mistaken for learning; schools have more control over teaching than learning, so when teachers are asked to be accountable, they mistakenly assume that they should do more teaching. The assumption here is that learning takes place only when the teacher is talking. If students are talking to each other, they are considered "discipline problems." A far more sensible arrangement is for the faculty to be organized into staff teams consisting of credentialed professionals as well as noncertified experts available to respond to specific needs of students, individually or in appropriate task groups. Teams have the flexibility needed to reorganize, reallocate, and redesign in the interest of students' achieving optional learning.

Staff teams provide a vehicle for organizing cross-aged groups representing at least two but often three grade levels. Many teachers report that cross-aging proves more responsive to the learning demands of individual students. A strength of cross-aging students is peer teaching, an improved resource for peer tutoring, peer mentoring, and peer counselling. It is high time that schools take advantage of the availability of peer teaching in which students who have mastered certain skills assist those who have not.

When students work in pairs or small groups to help each other more, they develop sophisticated cognitive strategies which result in higher achievement. In learning situations directed by staff teams, student progress is measured by performance (know how, know why, and can do) rather than on the basis of age or time engaged. Learning time is based upon the variability of students' tasks and needs rather than a fixed schoolwide schedule. Team talents must be balanced nicely between the diversity of individual professional roles, which include roles as coaches, facilitators, and focused didactive instructors. The most popular type of team consists of lead teachers, assistant teachers, and paraprofessionals.

It does not seem to be true that reforms aimed at the above-average students trickle down to at-risk youth. There is, however, evidence that the reverse of this process takes place as reforms that work for the bottom half of the class radiate up to the above average students. Teacher teams coupled with peer teaching are better able to adapt this reform principle than individual teachers working with a single class. Team teaching is beginning to be an acceptable and improved practice by even the most conventional teachers.

MODEL FOR CHANGE

How does a conventional elementary school go about the process of changing to a nongraded organization with teachers operating in teams instead of as individuals?

Research into how change can be brought about in schools (Colorado State Department of Education 1990) offers a model which any school can use to initiate this and other reforms.

The model assumes that in every school, at one end of the faculty spectrum, there is a "critical mass" of "productively dissonant" staff who are willing to leave the comfort zone of the status quo and experiment with new ideas.

The "critical mass" of an individual school's staff, in concert with its pricipal's leadership and an active parent support base, can begin a pilot phase and start a chain reaction which will radically change the school. How many is a "critical mass"? The numbers are nearly always small. As a group they are mindful that many of their students have educational needs which are not being addressed. They are aware that tinkering with the system through conventional staff development courses will not transform the curriculum and instruction on behalf of the students. It is up to the principal to move with those who are ready to go, and at the same time take care not to alienate or polarize other staff.

At the opposite end of the "critical mass" spectrum is an unyielding small group that is deeply entrenched in doing things as they have always done them. Strongly opposed to the view of the "critical mass," this small number of staff takes continuing comfort in remaining as experts within the territory they term as their classroom. Although they may argue for fewer students, more materials, and a reduction of regulations, they adamantly oppose any disruption of the status quo. Their view of the system is that it is working adequately.

In between these two extreme groups and making up the middle ground are a majority of staff, open to change, but cautious as to how it will affect them. This key group must be given time to think through the implications and details of changes from the present routine which are proposed by the "critical mass." Given time and a zone of comfort, once the middle staff sorts out the meaning of change and its value to them, they eventually become responsive to what reform can do for students and for themselves.

Consequently, it makes sense to begin reform with that group of teachers making up the "critical mass." They should be provided freedom and support while the remainder of the staff observes, discusses, considers, and agrees not to "shoot the new reforms out of the saddle prematurely."

The dynamics of the discrepancies between what schools are doing and what they can conceivably do when they clarify their values and develop them into visions is a very exciting possibility. While most schools have a mission statement which has been developed by a faculty committee, schools seldom develop a vision of a learning environment which will serve pupils who will live most of their lives in the twenty-first century. The school's vision statement should be a joint action of teachers and parents who are the key stakeholders in the school's outcomes. Since education is too important to leave up to the educators and too complex to leave up to the nonprofessionals, a mix of parents and educators provides the best resource for vision statements.

CHAPTER 4

Dilemmas of the Elementary Schools' Curricula

What must emerge as a landmark of today's schools is a widespread concern for quality and the intellectual renewal of education. This calls for an unprecedented participation by university scholars and scientists in the development of a new mathematics and science curriculum for the elementary schools.

In the past the shaping of the elementary school curriculum has been dominated by college of education professors. Since they have been the key figures in the training of teachers, their influence has inundated the process of teaching and learning in elementary school classrooms.

But this ascendancy is on the wane and will continue to decline. Evidence of the deterioration of the professors' influence is seen in the action of twenty-six states which have adopted alternative plans for certifying as teachers individuals who have taken no education courses. A recent conference in Washington sponsored by the U.S. Department of Education reported this trend is spreading to all states.

Even more dramatic proof of the debility of colleges of education happened recently when the nation's new National Board for Professional Teaching Standards, which was established to set high and rigorous standards for what teachers need to know and do, decided not to require any education courses as a prerequisite to becoming a Board Certified Teacher.

These two significant events portend a radical shift away from pedagogy courses as a requirement for teaching, and a significant decline in the influence of educational psychology on teaching and learning. The impact of this convulsive change will leave its mark. What is called for is a loosening of entrenched orthodoxies of pedagogy, which will in turn unleash fresh mandates for a more enlightened approach to quality education.

The first new mandate is the demand to make the curriculum more rigorous throughout the elementary school, but especially in the early years. It is here that colleges of education have done the most damage through their insistence that kindergartens avoid serious learning and concentrate on the social development of the child. The notion that the best curriculum for children of age five is one of social activities has, for too long, held its grip on the nation's kindergartens.

THE RESEARCHERS AND READINESS FOR LEARNING

The irrelevant hypothesis that children cannot learn intellectual ideas at an early age was refuted by the distinguished scholar of intelligence J. McVicker Hunt, who conducted one of the most extensive reviews of research ever done on intellectual development. In his historic book, *Intelligence and Experience*, Hunt reprimanded social development theories when he wrote:

> The counsel from experts on child rearing during the third and most of the fourth decades of the twentieth century to let children be while they grow and to avoid excessive stimulation was highly unfortunate (Hunt 1961).

Hunt concluded that during the early years children must be helped to achieve at a substantially faster rate of intellectual capacity.

Hunt's conclusions on the need for an earlier emphasis on intellectual development for children correspond with those of the noted Harvard psychologist Jerome Bruner, who wrote,

> Experience over the past decade points to the fact that our schools may be wasting precious years by postponing the teaching of many important subjects on the ground that they are too difficult (Bruner 1963, 12).

Bruner dropped the other shoe with the startling proposition that "any subject may be taught to anybody at any age in some form" (Bruner 1963, 40).

His basic conclusions about learning at an early age have enormous implications for reforming the elementary school curricula: "As far as I am concerned, young children learn almost everything faster than adults do if it can be given to them in terms they understand (Bruner 1963, 40). He explains that this calls for respecting the ways of thought of the growing child and being courteous enough to translate material into logical forms, tempting him to advance:

> Then it is possible to introduce him at an early age to the ideas and styles that in later life make an educated man. We might ask, as a criterion for any subject taught in primary school whether, when fully developed, it is worth an adult's knowing, and whether having known it as a child makes a person a better adult. If the answer to both questions is negative or ambiguous, then the material is cluttering the curriculum. If the hypothesis with which this section was introduced is true that any subject can be taught effectively to any child in some intellectually honest form, then it should follow that a curriculum ought to be built around the great issues, principles and values that a society deems as worthy of the continual concern of its members (Bruner 1963, 52).

Bruner also has superb advice for curriculum development with the assertion that:

> The first and most obvious problem is how to construct curricula that can be taught by ordinary teachers to ordinary students and at the same time reflect clearly the basic subject or underlying principles of various fields of inquiry. The problem is two fold: first, how to have the basic subjects rewritten and their teaching materials revamped in such a way that the pervading and powerful ideas and attitudes relating to them are given a central role: second how to match the levels of these materials to capacities of

students of different abilities at different grades in school (Bruner 1973, 70).

For more than three decades, scholars of intelligence have called for increased intellectual activity in kindergartens, but they have been voices crying in education's considerable forests of ignorance. Colleges of education and their insistence on social development have been the prevailing influence.

An examination of the present curriculum, particularly as it is practiced in the early grades, makes it abundantly clear that the influence of the colleges of education has spelled disaster for elementary education. The only way out of this morass is to put the best minds in any particular discipline to work on the task of determining what should be taught and at what level. The decision as to what should be taught to elementary school children in science, arithmetic, geography, and history must be made with the aid of those with a high degree of vision and competence in each of those fields.

In literature there has long been a body of knowledge which is fascinating to children, if the schools will just use it. *Aesop's Fables, Grimm's Fairy Tales,* and *Mother Goose* lead a variety of selections which are ideal for teaching young children to read for pleasure and enjoyment. The emphasis in grades K through 2 should be on instilling in children a love of reading. This means getting away from the present concentration on skill development. Once children are taught to read, the next two years should be spent in teaching them to read for enjoyment.

INFLATED TEST SCORES

Consider the scandal of the Cannell report three years ago: Dr. Cannell, a West Virginia physician, developed a distrust for norm referenced achievement test results when troubled school patients of his failed in school, but earned above average test scores. Cannell conducted a private survey (1987) and found that all fifty states claimed to be above average in school achievement.

Subsequently, the U.S. Office of Educational Research and

Improvement funded a study to examine Dr. Cannell's findings and confirmed that all of the states that administer norm referenced tests do indeed report more than 50 percent of their students to be above the national average in attainment.

Similarly, data from local school districts paint a rosy picture of achievement. For example, 65 percent of all school districts report that their students are reading above average in the third grade. This euphoric picture of accomplishment points to questionable practices of teaching to the test. The outcome is a major source of inflated test score reporting.

THE GREAT READING DEBATE

For the past fifty years America's classrooms have been used by educational psychologists and educationists as a laboratory for unproven theories of learning. This educational malpractice has resulted in a near collapse of public education.

During this time educators have debated, with no sensible conclusions, the best way to teach the schools' most basic subject, reading. To the increasing frustration of parents and the general public, elementary schools continue to be the battleground between educator advocates of phonics who stress letters and sounds versus those who argue for the strategy called whole language methodology. Instead of one method gaining acceptance over the years, the debate has continued to escalate among reading educators with the primary schools caught in the middle, hopelessly confused over which procedure to use.

Numerous education topics draw heated debates but the controversy over the first R has been the most vehement and the most visible for years. This argument has spilled over into school boards, state legislatures and even the halls of the U.S. Congress. While arguments about how to teach children to read continue to rage within the education research community, on Capitol Hill, in business, and in the classroom, illiteracy continues to be the nation's most critical education problem.

In an effort to make some sense out of "the great reading controversy," Congress passed legislation in 1981 requiring the Department of Education to research the matter of the best method for teaching reading and to provide parents, teachers, and the general public with a guide for determining an effective reading program.

The outcome was a typical bureaucratic response. Four years after the mandate, the Department of Education published a six hundred page research report (*Becoming A Nation of Readers 1985*) which it said, "examined research on beginning reading in search of a common ground on this divisive topic." The study concluded that the schools should achieve a balance between the phonics approach and whole word reading methodology.

Members of congress were outraged to receive another research report with no clear conclusions. Their vexation can be appreciated when one considers the estimate of the International Reading Association that research reports on illiteracy are currently being prepared at the rate of one thousand per year.

Senator Edward Zorinsky of Nebraska, who sponsored the original legislation, died before the four year study was finished but his former aide commented on the outcome, "A massive research report is not helpful to parents and the general public in determining effective programs" (Education Week 2/7/90).

Legislation was promptly introduced by some members of Congress to hold hearings as to why the Department of Education did not follow the Congressional mandate. Additional proposed legislation will require the department to meet its obligation.

While Congress fumes, the debate over methods is becoming more polarized and escalating to a full scale academic war. The arguments are so fierce that there is little hope of quelling the dispute and finding agreement on the best method of teaching reading.

Leaders in methods of teaching reading are college of education professors who prepare teachers for the classroom. The reading dispute is just another sad episode in the miserable failure of the professors of education to provide intelligent leadership on problems of learning.

Reducing the argument to its simplest terms, the whole language movement advocates reading whole texts rather than parts of words. Its supporters believe that focusing on reading mechanics, as the phonics method does, impedes children's ability to read. They contend that the emphasis on skills is atomistic and takes away the meaning and fun of reading.

Phonics advocates, on the other hand, contend that children being taught phonetically recognize words quicker and faster and comprehend better. Leading phonics champion Jean Chall of the Harvard Reading Clinic blames the decline in the use of phonics for the sharp drop in performance in reading achievement of nine-year-olds between 1984 and 1986.

As the schools become increasingly desperate over the poor performance of students in reading achievement, the two sides have become intractable, each accusing the other of grandstanding with soap box oratory rather than calmness and good sense. Showing scant regard for the dilemma of schools which are struggling to teach reading, the professors of reading education continue their grandiloquence, stoking the fires of incendiary rhetoric with little concern for reason.

In the meantime the schools wrestle with more mundane obstacles to the learning and practice of reading. Francie M. Alexander, associate superintendent for California, says:

> We're fighting the wrong enemy. The real enemies are Nintendo and Saturday morning cartoons. They are the enemies of the cultural literacy we need (*Education* Week 3/21/90).

The tension between the two groups over method continues to accelerate, baffling the nation's elementary schools on how to accomplish the single most important function they are mandated to perform, the teaching of reading.

The relevant question is, "Why does America have a reading problem in the first place?" We are an affluent and technologically advanced nation. We have compulsory education to age sixteen and it is free.

The problem lies within the network of state owned and operated teachers' colleges which cannot agree on the best way to teach reading. Unquestionably teaching children to read is the most important objective educators have to accomplish. Reading is a prerequisite for everything else, both in the school and in life itself. Not knowing the answer to the question of "best method," the education professionals have engaged in a form of educational malpractice as they persist in training teachers in methods about which they themselves cannot agree.

Phonics advocates contend that students should first learn the alphabet, then the sounds of each letter, how the letters are blended to form syllables, and how these syllables make up words. As a matter of routine practice, teachers need to include systematic code-oriented instruction in the primary grades. Phonics facilitates word identification and fast accurate identification as a necessary condition for comprehension. The child learns the mechanics of reading and when he is through, he can read.

By contrast, the whole language approach teaches that children should memorize or guess at words in context by using initial letter or picture clues. In the whole language approach to reading, children are not taught the fundamental structure of language. Instead they become engaged in what Dr. Kenneth Goodman, one of the leading proponents of the whole language approach, calls a psycholinguistic guessing game.

Since the experts are unable to agree on how to teach reading, it is no wonder that the nation has a serious literacy problem. How much money is being spent by the federal government on the illiteracy problem is anybody's guess, but fourteen different federal agencies operate seventy-nine different literacy programs.

An analysis of the reading tests administered by the National Assessment of Educational Progress indicates that where elementary children fall behind is in comprehending what they are reading. The solution seems to be to introduce literature soon after children learn to read in order to move them at an earlier age towards the skills of understanding.

In the absence of any kind of consensus, schools choose one method or another without really knowing whether they are using the best method. It is no wonder that achievement in reading by American children is abysmal. And it is easy to understand why large numbers of children reach the third grade without being able to read.

One of the major obstacles to serious and dramatic reform of reading instruction comes from ingrained professional organizations which oppose new approaches to the problem. For example, the National Assessment for Educational Progress (the nation's report card) is planning an assessment of fourth grade reading in 1992 which will provide the first state by state comparison of what children have learned. The plan is to establish a benchmark which will give useful data to state and national policy makers.

Surprisingly, the nation's leading reading organization, the International Reading Association, has come out vigorously against state by state comparisons. This is just another irresponsible example of educators fearing to face up to the outcomes of their teaching and attempting to hide deficiencies from the general public.

State by state data on learning is essential, since states have the responsibility for education and are desperately trying to improve schools. If a state does not know where it stands in comparison to other states, then what is it to use as a benchmark for improving its educational system?

Reading is the key that opens up the entire learning process. Elementary schools must energize intensive reading programs and reading must be taught well and taught right.

TELEVISION AND CHILDREN

In examining possible explanations for the perplexingly low performance of elementary children in every state (National Assessment of Mathematics 1991) the study found that children who watch a great deal of television performed especially low.

Educators have long regarded television viewing by children as a major obstacle in their effort to wrestle the education system into condition to do its part in meeting the cognitive learning needs of a modern society.

Children brought up on television often have serious difficulty adjusting to the more passive instruction of the classroom. Researchers in literacy and the problems of teaching reading are beginning to point a finger at Children's Workshop program "Sesame Street" as a cause of students' inattention and frustration in school (Healy 1991).

Many researchers now believe that the program is no

more than a circus of activity with an adverse effect on literacy and learning to read. The charge: the program is noisy, fast paced, and visually demanding with abrupt and cacophonous sounds to get the viewer's attention. This frenetic activity is considered to be a direct cause of the syndrome that students increasingly cannot listen, pay attention in school, or apply themselves to lessons that demand persistence.

After twenty years of ballyhooing its success, "Sesame Street" producers came close to becoming an emblem of immortality in early childhood education. Recently, however, the production has come under spirited attack from early childhood education critics who charge that it does far more harm than good.

While early studies of "Sesame Street" claimed miraculous success in teaching disadvantaged children to recognize letters and numerals, current research on how young children should be introduced to reading conclusively refutes the methods used in the program. Furthermore, the results of success in the early studies of "Sesame Street" are now being challenged as meager, not worth the huge expenditures, and not based on research as to how children should be introduced to reading. The executives of the program freely admit that their research has concentrated on "what makes children watch" rather than "the achievement of outcomes" (*Education Week* 9/19/90).

Reading teachers and researchers alike contend that the production, instead of helping, undermines the teaching of reading which requires time, thought, and practice, by embedding letters in a whirlwind of activity of visual events, noise, and slapstick comedy. The program uses techniques of fast movement, sudden noises, and bright color to capture and maintain the attention of young children. The characters talk too fast and topics are shifted abruptly.

Leading psychologist Jane M. Healy, after extensive viewing of the program, refers to it as "surface glitz, . . . a peripatetic carnival of on-screen activity." In her words,

> Twenty years of throwing dancing words at children is producing exactly what we might expect: Students who, even when they learn to sound out the words, find reading "boring," who

Dilemmas of the Elementary Schools' Curricula 57

can't understand why meaning doesn't magically appear like a special effect and who give up when it doesn't. . . . Reading is a complex intellectual act that cannot be peddled like an educational toy.

A brain brought up on a steady diet of noisy fast paced visually demanding programs like "Sesame Street" is physically different and thus is equipped differently for learning than a brain which has gotten its intellectual nourishment primarily from personally absorbing play, social interactions with peers, and intelligent conversation with real adults. In fact, there is every reason to believe that "Sesame Street" type programing is related to the fact that teachers increasingly complain that their students: can't listen, can't pay attention in class; can't apply themselves to problems that demand persistence.

I believe it is not coincidence that our faith in puppets as teachers has presaged a major decline in reading and learning skills. Uncritical acceptance of a program like "Sesame Street" as a model for "education" has started a generation of children in the seductive school of organized silliness, where their first lesson is that learning is something adults can be expected to make happen for them as quickly and pleasantly as possible. Thus prepared, they can hardly be blamed if they fail to discover for themselves the personal joys, time consuming as they are, of serious learning, mental effort, and mastery. (Healy 1991)

In addition, other critics express alarm over the effect on the ethics of children viewing the program (*Education Week* 9/19/90). Children and puppets are being constantly put in embarrassing situations, made fun of, and laughed at; children eavesdrop or peep through keyholes, and meanness is glorified. Frequently derogatory remarks about a character are presented as funny and often actions have no consequences. Also characters often receive offensive putdowns. Perhaps the most serious offense of "Sesame Street" is that it misleads children about how print behaves and exposes them to incidental bits of knowledge without connecting and linking learning to reasoning skills.

After examining the research and viewing the programs, one can only conclude that "Sesame Street" is an idea whose time has come and faded. In the interest of better preschool preparation this farce should be discontinued.

CHILDREN AND TELEVISION: A POLICY STATEMENT

While much has been said and written about the effects of television viewing on children, one of the boldest, most impressive disclosures is contained in a 1990 policy statement on the subject from the American Academy of Pediatrics. The academy's document warned pediatricians and parents in straightforward language about the devastating effects of excessive television on children's development.

A major purpose of the academy was to convey in written policy, alarm about the influence of television in promoting violent and aggressive behaviors, early sexual activity, and alcohol and drug abuse. In addition to the psychological danger to children, the policy statement cautioned that passive viewing contributes substantially to obesity.

The Academy's policy memorandum directed attention to Neilson data which established that children from two to five years of age view approximately twenty-five hours per week, children age six to eleven watch more than twenty-two hours per week, and adolescents twelve to, seventeen watch twenty-three hours weekly. It advised parents to limit their children's television viewing to one or two hours per day and encouraged them to develop television substitutes such as reading, instructive hobbies, and athletics.

The policy statement expressed concern over the estimated 14,000 sexual references and innuendoes per year on television which obviously contribute to the increasing frequency of adolescent pregnancy and sexually transmitted diseases. It urged that parents adopt a role of supervision and selectivity.

In the strongest of terms, pediatricians support legislation making broadcast of high quality children's programing a condition of license renewal. They also seek legislation mandating one hour per day of programs of educational benefit to children.

Unquestionably, television has enormous influence on ele-

Dilemmas of the Elementary Schools' Curricula 59

mentary school age children. Programs viewed should be carefully selected by parents and kept to a minimum. The school and its curricula are best supported by parents who see that their children read extensively and who become involved in their children's homework.

In the first state by state assessment of learning, North Dakota ranked at the top of the national rankings. The overview report (National Assessment For Educational Progress) found it significant that North Dakota also ranked at the top in the low rate of television viewing by children.

Cognitive science suggests that children learn best when they are taught in the context of situations, activities, and problems. Learning in context breaks down the barriers between knowledge and practice and far surpasses the formal approach to learning and the resulting mismatch between students and learning which exists in today's schools.

To change elementary education at the level necessary, appropriate outcome measures must be in place and instruction built on an understanding of real world situations.

HOME-SCHOOLING

Nationwide, increasing numbers of parents are not sending their children to the public schools, choosing instead to educate them at home. One of the most often cited reasons is to protect children from the peer-dominated culture of the public schools.

No data is available on the number of children being educated at home. Too many school systems consider the practice of home-schooling a reflection on their competence and go out of their way to ignore the problem. Consequently, they keep no records of children being educated at home by their parents. However, the numbers are large and growing.

The impact of the home-schooling phenomenon affects the elementary schools more profoundly than secondary schools, as parents generally feel more comfortable teaching the curriculum of the earlier years. They are much less inclined to take on secondary school home-schoolers.

Most home-schooling families want nothing more from

the school system than to be left alone. But increasing numbers of home-schoolers have brought a number of California communities to recognize that discretion is the better part of valor. Since so many parents are educating their children at home, schools are beginning to offer home-schooling families annual expense accounts of $1,000 for educational materials.

Parents may apply for this subsidy for such educational expenses as books, computers, software, foreign language tapes, crayons, museum trips, and even ballet lessons. The school districts' purchasing departments review the parents' receipts for these items and reimburse them for these and other predefined expenses.

California is not the only state becoming friendlier towards home-schooling. In Arizona's 1990 elections, a major candidate for state school superintendent ran on a platform that would stop the hassling of home-schooling parents by local school districts. Virginia legislators, who were on the verge of cracking down on home-schooling in the mid-1980's, found themselves confronted by testimony from a group of poised, articulate thirteen-year-olds who had never been enrolled in public school. They quickly backed down.

While California programs are daring and innovative, California school districts are undermining home-schooling in its purest sense by attempting to become involved with parents in order that their school districts can obtain a substantial state subsidy. Parents who cooperate are required to make monthly reports and meet three times a year with a school principal. The school justifies the subsidy of $1,000 it gives to parents by listing the home-schooling children with the state as being in an independent study program sponsored by the school. For every child who is switched from pure home-schooling to a school's contrived independent study program, the school receives approximately $3000 from the state. While this is a good deal for the schools, Connie Pfeil of the Northern California Home-schooling Association warns,

> The subtle but constant pressure from the system to conform and produce acceptable levels of paper work suggests that maybe home-schooling and the public school system are simply incompatible at a very basic level (*Wall Street Journal* 6/10/90).

Frank Clark, who administers a home-schooling program for Cupertino, California, school district, puts the issue in perspective:

> Schools are going to become more like business, if they can't satisfy parents they will go away (*Wall Street Journal* 6/10/90).

The crux of the matter is that home-schooling is on the rise nationwide. As consumers have learned to be more alert to their rights, more people have bought into the notion that the squeakier the wheel, the better the grease. In any event, increasing numbers of Americans are becoming aware that the environment of the home is superior to that of the school as a place of learning.

CHAPTER 5

A Reform Response to the Learning Deficit

When the issue of elementary reform is discussed, the first question to be asked is, "How effective is the present system?" In the traditional school, one teacher is assigned a group of from twenty-five to thirty students. The typical classroom has windows on one side and chalkboards on the other three walls. Most of the action takes place at the chalkboards. In this arena, educational efficiency is at capacity and still far below expectations. Wringing more productivity out of an elementary school classroom is not going to be easy. Resistance to change is formidable. This makes it imperative that schools begin the search for a new and more innovative model to replace the conventional elementary school style of teaching and learning.

To visualize the problem, one need look no further than the curriculum of the primary school (K-3), which has been homogenized, diluted, and diffused to the point that it no longer has a central purpose. In effect, the entire curriculum of early education is like a smorgasbord in which the appetizers and desserts are frequently mistaken for the main course.

Radical reform of the elementary schools is rapidly becoming the nation's highest educational priority. The most important subjects in the elementary school are reading and mathematics, yet these are the subjects with which the schools are least effective. Research data is clear that many children leave the elementary school unable to read and do simple computations. This deplorable outcome is no longer acceptable.

Beginning with kindergarten, the elementary school curriculum must be reformed to accomplish its purpose of achieving satisfactory outcomes in reading and mathematics for all children. Entirely too many children are not learning these skills and consequently are falling by the wayside. Central to the search for a new elementary school model is the premise that if the quality of education in America is to be vastly improved, elementary students need better instruction in math and science and at an earlier age.

SCHOOL DIVERSITY AND CHOICE

The major reform being pushed by the Bush administration deals with the matter of giving parents the right to choose the schools which their children will attend. The fallacy in the idea of choice is the pervasive sameness in the nation's public elementary schools. There is such a paucity of diversity that there is literally nothing to choose from. The elementary school on Elmwood Street is no different from the one on Tanglewood Avenue. Choice has little meaning if there are no attractive goods to choose from. Therefore, the notion is flawed that parental choice among public schools will promote quality education. So, while there is a great deal of talk going on about the need to give parents a choice of schools and subsequently become more involved in their children's education, the vast majority of school districts and individual schools are designed and operated in a way that effectively excludes parents from either making choices or having a meaningful voice in the education of their children.

The established structure and methods of traditional school organization and operation are simply not crafted to comply with educational choice. Indeed most public schools, given their rigid habits of operation, are and must inevitably be uncomfortable with reforms of diversity and choice.

In order to penetrate the nation's rigidly organized teacher workforce, a more powerful innovation than the tepid concept of choice among public schools needs to be introduced. Choice among look-alike schools insulated by union power against change is very timid tinkering with a fundamentally flawed machine.

In spite of the inappropriateness of choosing among look-alikes, when the voice of the president and the leaders of corporate America commend and glorify choice as a force that will dramatically reform public education, the public responds hypnotically. But the legendary phrase, "What's good for General Motors, is good for the country," is wearing thin, and not just in the world of automobiles. It is certainly no panacea when applied to schools.

Well-intentioned ideas from corporate board rooms assume that competition in the marketplace is a phenomenon which applies to schools just as it does to business. They assume that parents can and should shop around for schools and make choices just as they do for furniture, television sets, and groceries. High level political and business support for choice has created a bandwagon type of situation with much hoopla in which parents are looking forward to shopping around and choosing the school which their children will attend.

There is nothing wrong with educational choice, if there is something to choose from. But public elementary schools, as they are presently operated, are the same everywhere. There is not a dime's worth of difference between the elementary schools of Maine and those of California. Unfortunately, the advocates of choice among public schools have created a choice program out of thin air. Choosing between lousy schools is not choice, and there are far more lousy schools than good ones. The notion of choice, without including private schools, is just one more "quick fix," perhaps best described as a politically attractive myth.

Choice, leaving out the private school option, is not a panacea as its advocates would have the public believe. It is not even a mechanism for major school improvement. At best it is a peripheral reform. It is certainly not worthy of the bandwagon hysteria and hoopla which it has generated.

As the distinguished researcher James Coleman put it,

> Public schools have become increasingly impersonal agents of a larger society. schools have lost their capacity to support and sustain the family in its task of raising children. In reality, they

have lost their claim to be a community of interest with families. The restoration of schools requires abandoning the assumption of the school as an agent of the state and substituting an assumption that the school is properly an extension of the family (Coleman 1985).

The research is even more vociferous in denouncing the present system of public school organization. Coons and Sugarman deplore the "central control" of schools, which they call a formula for stagnation, unresponsiveness, and mediocrity:

> Their incentive to innovate is meager and their capacity to terminate unsuccessful programs is as bad or worse (Coons and Sugarman 1978).

The primary method of assigning students to schools has historically been by geographic residence; students are expected to attend the school established for them in the neighborhood area of their local school district. This arbitrary assignment for school attendance protects schools from changing because it effectively eliminates any kind of marketplace. In order for the practice of choice to be effective, students should be able to choose between public and private schools with the money allocated for their public school education following them to the private setting. Recent research from the Rand Corporation found that disadvantaged students perform better in parochial schools than public schools.

Giving parents a choice between public and private schools is a reform strategy aimed at forcing a more effective, efficient, and long overdue restructuring of public elementary and secondary schools. For the system to work, choices developed and offered by school districts must be distinctive and clearly denote different kinds of schools rather than minor variations on the standard model. Further, the choice program offered must be carefully crafted with controls to ensure that poor and minority children have equal access to all of the choices including private and parochial schools and that every school of choice ends up with a student body, a parent body, and a staff that is roughly representative of the school district's population as a whole.

An outcome of the choice innovation is to create a student

body whose members are alike in some educationally important way. This requires a differentiation among the various schools within a district, permitting students and their families to select the type of school that interests them most. Parental choice as a reform is highly compatible with the reforms of flexibility, autonomy, accountability, and site empowerment. The latter reform gives local groups of teachers and principals more responsibility for figuring out their problems and makes them accountable for programs and the resulting amount of achievement in their particular school. This concept also calls for increased involvement of parents in school decision making.

Initiating parental choice, diversifying schools, and giving local schools increased autonomy are reforms which are long overdue. Barriers to participating in these reforms need to be removed by the various state legislatures. Once that action in taken, schools can be reformed around new and innovative curricula.

In summary, if the concept of choice is going to meaningful, then there must be a clear difference in schools. In the public arena parents should be able to choose among different types of schools including small schools and other flexible environments. The inclusion of private and parochial schools with the money following the students makes the prerogative to select a school a viable notion.

LENGTHENING THE ELEMENTARY SCHOOL DAY

Lengthening the school day and diversifying the curricula in the added-on time is the most promising suggestion to date for creating schools which are notably different one from the other. The significant components of the elementary school are the curriculum, the instruction, and the length of the day. These fundamentals, at the present time, are geared to accommodate children from homes in which the father is working and mother remains at home. Since fewer than 25 percent of the nation's families now fit this category, it is time for the elementary schools to redevelop and redesign their programs to more effectively cope with a student body which has less parenting.

Nationwide, nearly 75 percent of children attending elementary schools currently come from families in which there is a working single parent or both parents are in the work force. The result is that "latch key" children are now legion. This compels a reexamination of all the components of schooling to assure that schools are responsive to the population they serve.

Longer days for schools as visualized here represent a natural, innovative move away from the currently outdated school response to the family lifestyle where only the father is working and the mother remains in the home. Since this lifestyle is passing, schools must make a more relevant response to the emerging new lifestyles of families. The intact family with a mother at home is now rare; consequently motivated children ready to learn are rare. Children from broken homes face a plethora of stresses that the schools are too quick to gloss over and dismiss as irrelevant to the learning process.

The idea of elementary schools with lengthened days was extrapolated from the magnet school notion of being more accommodating to the needs of the schools' demography. Longer day schools feature the same strategies of magnetism as magnet schools, including special subject area focus, diverse teaching strategies, and extended day instruction. Their great strength lies in the learning opportunities available in a 33 percent longer school day.

One thing should be clear: extra hours in the school day do not mean more of the same. A mere stretching of the traditional curriculum is the last thing the school should do in the effort to improve. The purpose of the lengthened day is to assure that all children get all the help they need to be successful in reading, mathematics, and science. A high priority of the lengthened hours of school is to pay special attention to average students and give them a new lease on learning. While the development and the organization of schools with lengthened days may seen like an extreme departure from current elementary school programing, it must be borne in mind that the organization and curricula of conventional elementary schools are in need of constructive turbulence.

In the afternoon program a major suggested technique is "cooperative learning," a teaching strategy whereby students are divided into groups and teach one another. If students can learn from one another, they can also learn from teachers who are not certified. This approach brings a new dimension to the threshold of teaching and learning.

A NEW TIME FRAME FOR SCHOOLING

All fifty states require their elementary schools to operate on a six to six and a half hour school day. Consequently, typical elementary schools function from approximately 8:00 A.M. until 2:30 P.M. Under a new and innovative proposed time schedule, when the traditional day is over at 2:30 P.M., no buses will leave to take the children home, and the extended day program will commence. The school then offers afternoon programing organized around a particular subject theme until 5:30 P.M. The mission is highly focused on improving students' performance and attitudes.

Schools which take into consideration the needs of the nation, after setting up an extensive reading program for grades K-2, will develop an afternoon curriculum which revolves around science. The science theme should be based entirely upon "hands on" experiments. Other components of the extended day science activity are mathematics, including estimation skills, reading which varies from free reading in the library to tutorial instruction, aerobics, and counseling.

In addition to focusing on a theme, the extended day is an ideal time to both teach the gifted and zero in on high risk students through special counseling and remedial instruction.

School buses at extended day schools will take the children home only at 5:30 P.M.; however, families with only one of the parents employed may want their children in school no longer than the regular school day. These parents will have the prerogative of picking up their youngsters when the regular school day ends at 2:30, or at 3:30, or at 4:30. Their children have the choice of participating in none, part, or all of the longer day.

Suggested subject areas of focus for the extended day school are:

Mathematics
Reading
History
Geography
Performing Arts
Music
Foreign Language
Sports

Briefly, the extended day elementary school is designed to accomplish the following purposes:

- Have a longer day in order to increase instruction time.
- Accommodate single parents and families with both parents working by providing a safe and appropriate environment when no one is at home.

Theme Centered Kindergarten Through Grade 3
2:30–5:30 P.M. Daily

In kindergarten through grade 3 the major emphasis must be on increased reading and mathematics instruction. Although a number of themes are relevant in grades 4 through 6, the only theme germane to the primary grades is one which focuses on reading with an allocation of time for arithmetic. The following subject themes presented are suggested with the caveat that they will be modified by implementing schools to reflect the interests of parents, needs of students, and concerns of teaching staff.

Reading as a Theme
K through 3

2:30–3:30	Reading	Library	Listening
3:30–4:00	Math	Math	Math
4:00–5:00	Reading	Library	Listening
5:00–5:30	Writing	Writing	Writing

A Reform Response to the Learning Deficit

While reading is the only appropriate theme for the primary grades, it is also pertinent as an area of focus in grades 4 through 6. Other applicable Themes for these grades are described below.

Theme Centered Curricula for Grades 4 through 6
2:30–5:30 P.M. Daily

Science as a Theme

2:30–3:30	Science
3:30–4:00	Math
4:00–5:00	Reading
5:00–5:30	Aerobics

History as a Theme

2:30–3:30	American History
3:30–4:30	European History
4:30–5:30	World History

Mathematics as a Theme

2:30–3:30	Advanced Math	Regular Math	Tutoring Math
3:30–4:30	Library Reading	Reading Instruction	Tutoring Reading
4:30–5:30	Aerobics	Aerobics	Aerobics

Geography as a Theme

2:30–3:30	Geography
3:30–4:30	Reading
4:30–5:30	Aerobics

Foreign Language as a Theme

        2:30–3:30   Oriental Languages
        3:30–4:30   Aerobics
        4:30–5:30   Spanish

North Carolina is currently the only state with a requirement that all kindergarten students study and practice a foreign language; however, a trend is developing. Georgia has a pilot program for fifteen school districts, and the state board of education has approved making the program statewide by 1996. Maryland is piloting some programs, and Oklahoma has mandated that all elementary students be taught a foreign language by 1993.

Hi Tech as a Theme

        2:30–3:30   Computer
        3:30–4:30   Reading
        4:30–5:30   Aerobics

Performing Arts as a Theme

        2:30–3:30   Art
        3:30–4:30   Drama
        4:30–5:30   Dance

Music as a Theme

        2:30–3:30   Chorus
        3:30–4:30   Instrumental Music Practice
        4:30–5:30   Music History

Sports as a Theme

        2:30–3:30   Athletic Skills
        3:30–4:30   Reading
        4:30–5:30   Physical Fitness

A Reform Response to the Learning Deficit

While the author believes that Americans are too sports focused and does not recommend the selection of the sports theme, it is recognized that some parents may feel differently.

Theme-centered schools as proposed here are experimental schools which will constantly try new things. There are numerous combinations of subjects which can be scheduled, but the principal and teaching force of each school should decide on their particular mission after considering the school's demography and the interests of the parents of the children in attendance. It is anticipated that extended day programs will make use of computers and interactive video and concentrate on listening skills as an exciting new way to produce improved student achievement.

In planning for extended day programs, adequate provision should be made for recess breaks. While there has developed a national trend against recess in order to minimize problems such as children's disagreements and fights, a 1991 survey by the National Elementary Principal's Association supports school recess, saying it brings children back to the classroom more alert, calm, and productive. The advantage to the children of the breaks offsets the minor administrative problems caused during the breaks.

CHAPTER 6

How to "Guarantee" Student Achievement

State legislators, out of concern for the embarrassing declines in student achievement, have been throwing money at the educational problem. Salaries of school personnel have increased more than 77 percent since the 1981–82 school year. What has all of this money accomplished? Nothing, and the outlook for improving students' learning outcomes remains bleaker than ever as their achievement test scores continue in either a standstill or declining phase.

The data from a summary of twenty years of findings by the National Assessment of Educational Progress, a Congressionally funded assessment group covering eleven instructional areas, concludes, "Our present education performance is low and not improving" (The Reading Report Card 1967–1988). A six nation study released by the U.S. Office of Education in 1989 showed that American students ranked at or near the bottom in science and mathematics when compared to students from industrialized countries.

It is now time to shake the education establishment. State policy makers must establish clearly defined goals for student achievement and require that they be met. Constitutionally, education is a state responsibility and a local function. States provide roughly half the resources for elementary and secondary education while the balance comes from local governments operating under state authority. States have been dabbling in school reform for more than a decade without results. The time for vigorous action is at hand and the task is enormous. The challenge of the 90's is to focus on the elementary school and in so doing to provide learning environments that promote the success of children who are currently failing.

These objectives call for a process of state intervention when local school districts fail to improve learning. To assure accomplishment, strong new legislation is required spelling out specific points for intervention.

The following intervention practices aimed at the key levels of local policy and administration will have a profound affect on the outcomes of teaching and learning:

- School Board Members are disqualified from filing for reelection or reappointment to a second term if district achievement has not improved during their tenure of office. School board members unwilling to put the flag of student achievement high on their masthead should be removed from office. Measurement of achievement is determined by state assessment tests and based upon set goals for education in the form of core competencies. End of year and exit tests are based upon challenging subject matter emphasizing higher order skills in core subject areas.

- Superintendents may no longer be given four year contracts as is the case at present. All contracts are for two years and renewable based upon student outcomes. Superintendents are automatically dismissed when there is no improvement in student achievement after two years in office.

- School principals are employed on a two-year contract and reemployed based upon student achievement. Release is automatic if there is no overall school improvement during this period.

- Teachers are held accountable for outcomes in their classrooms and student achievement carefully monitored. When a teacher's students fail to meet projected outcomes, that teacher should be placed on probation and transferred to another situation. If the second group of students fails to meet expected outcomes, the teacher is replaced. Unlike today's achievement measures, the new tests for measuring outcomes are not exclusively multiple choice questions. They emphasize writing, reasoning, and demonstration of a student's ability to apply knowledge to solve problems. They are based upon clear and comparable objectives for schools regardless of where they are located.

The nation's leaders have established lofty national goals. Goals without student assessment standards and regularly monitored outcomes will be unattainable. The success of education must be judged on measurable outcomes of student learning, not just time spent in school. Intervention and removal of administrators and teachers whose students do not achieve is essential for rapid, no nonsense school reform. If the schools are to be quickly transformed into places of learning with accountability for learning outcomes, demonstrations of competency must be visible at every level.

The strategy for overhauling instruction and leadership so that employment is based upon student outcomes will seem extreme to the educational establishment which has never been expected to help all students achieve at high levels. But educators must assume new and more complex roles. First-rate educators are now critical to the success of each state's efforts to improve student outcomes.

The reforms we need cannot occur without changes in the way that local school districts operate. State policy makers must establish performance objectives for which school and district personnel must be held accountable. Only by taking drastic and turbulent action can the education system be made to respond to the challenges of the coming decade.

High expectations must be set for teachers and administrators, just as they are expected to set high expectations for all children. The linchpin of reform in the elementary schools rests on a bedrock belief that all children can learn at high levels. Students with special needs, or from poor and minority backgrounds, have long suffered from the unambitious expectations set for them in the public schools. Performance expectations for all students have been too low for too long. This is reflected in an unchallenging curriculum with distressing outcomes.

If the nation is to come even close to achieving the new national goals for education which have been set by the governors and the president, then we can no longer continue to tinker with an educational engine whose fundamental design is flawed. Dramatic changes in the performance of educators must be the canon of American education. Unswerving commitment to improvement, rather than maintaining the existing unproductive practices of school personnel, is required.

If the governors seriously believe their collective agreement that "America's educational performance must be second to none in the 21st century" (Education Summit 1989), then new and higher standards of performance are required for educators and must be rigidly enforced. The time for "wringing hands" and "oh dears" has passed. Somebody has to get tough or the war will be lost before the first battle begins.

STATE POLICY AND THE ELEMENTARY SCHOOL PRINCIPAL

As we approach the twenty-first century and the need to guarantee the learning of every child, society is troubled over the future of its schools but especially the quality of school leadership. This concern is not without cause as nothing less than the place of the United States among the community of nations is at stake.

A recent study by the Education Commission of the States concluded that state policy has very little to say about the principalship. For example, Ohio law specifies five duties for principals: (1) display the flag, (2) supervise student savings plans, (3) conduct drills, (4) keep records, (5) follow due process for student discipline (Pipo 1990). In brief, the role of the principal in many states is shaped by default. In practice, however, the principal should be the key person in the direction, operation, and learning outcomes of schooling.

In an era of school reform, ill-defined, nebulous, and obscure references to the duties of the schools' managers are in need of dramatic and perceptive change. Legislative energies should galvanize the principal's position into one of responsibility for the learning outcomes of the school. The principal should be accountable for learning and liable when it does not take place.

Principals should be employed only on the basis of performance contracts with continued employment contingent on the attainment of specified school performance. School boards, on their part, should aggressively identify and recruit bright and talented individuals from outside the education establishment to manage and direct their schools.

THE ELEMENTARY PRINCIPAL AS CEO

There is no reason why schools should not be run with the same efficiency and success as a well-orchestrated business firm. For this to happen, educators must adopt the corporate style of management. When schools are operated on businesslike principles, the principal functions with the power and vitality of a chief executive officer. As CEO of the school, he has the authority to give raises to good teachers and fire the bad ones. In addition, as CEO he must be held accountable for the learning outcomes of the school's students. If reading and math scores fail to maintain a high level, he should be released at the end of a two year contract. When this happens, he should not be eligible for another principal's position for a period of at least three years.

To achieve this type of dynamic organization, states must overhaul their antiquated education laws. For example, at present it is impossible for school managers to fire incompetent teachers. They just shuffle them from one location to another. It is now time for governors and legislators to bite the bullet, defy the teachers' unions, and employ and pay teachers on the basis of students' outcomes. Teachers who are able to produce high levels of achievement must be paid substantially more than those whose students' achievement improves only marginally.

Past experience shows that local school boards cannot face up to the unions and establish salary schedules on the basis of student performance. With an almost obsequious response to collective bargaining, local boards universally fail to take on the issue of different pay for different performance. Standardized salary schedules based upon seniority and reinforced by the collective bargaining process are to a considerable degree responsible for the continuing deterioration in the quality of the nation's teaching force. If this problem is to be dealt with, it must be handled by policy makers at the state level. Up to this point few governors have displayed the courage to take on the unions. Failure to cope with excessive and unreasonable demands have kept the educational establishment from achieving the flexibility which the public is now demanding. Until policy makers have the fortitude to tackle the union problem, it will be impossible for principals to act with the authority and responsibility of a chief executive officer. Legislation which will assure a higher caliber teaching force and differentiated pay based upon student outcomes should be implemented in all states and with all possible speed. No longer should the bottom one-third of the college-going population make up America's teaching force.

DISTRICT POLICY AND THE SUPERINTENDENT

Even more important than employing the elementary principal on a performance based contract, is the necessity to retain the district superintendent on the basis of how well the districts schools perform.

Superintendents should be hired, assessed, and fired on the basis of outcomes achieved by schools under their direction. The days of four-year contracts with no reference to the learning outcomes of students belong to a past era.

The absence of answerability for learning is conspicuous in the nation's school superintendents' contracts. Yesterday's complacent, self-satisfied administrators have no role to play in a new and exciting time of vitality in the schools. If learning outcomes are to improve dramatically, then the quality of school administration must change noticeably.

ACHIEVEMENT "GUARANTEED"

An important outcome of drastic reform is for school districts to be able to "guarantee" that all non-handicapped children who attend one of their elementary schools for six years will be at or above grade level as determined by state diagnostic tests. While this may seem like a radical suggestion at first glance, there is no reason why, following six years at a school, normal children are not at or above grade level, except for incompetence in instruction or administration, or both. Truly excellent schools will move at a faster clip and guarantee this level of achievement for students who attend the school for as few as three years.

The key to a guaranteed outcomes based curriculum reflecting improved instruction and developing student self-confidence is teacher collaboration. Under the present system, each child has the same teacher for one year. Those lucky enough to be in the class of an expert teacher are miles down the road while those across the hall under an incompetent teacher suffer from frustration and the loss of a year of learning. When teachers collaborate to guarantee learning outcomes, a team of three teachers is assigned to the same group of students for a three-year period. This arrangement spreads the talent around and minimizes the effects of mediocrity. Over a six-year period students will have worked with two different teams of teachers.

The other reform needed to guarantee the highest outcomes in achievement is to lengthen the elementary school year from the current 180 days of student attendance to 200 days.

While moving to a "results oriented" system may seem extreme at first glance, it is not unrealistic. The Commissioner of Education for New York state, Thomas Sobol, has outlined a similar plan (New York State Board of Regents Minutes 5/90). "Such a program is not for the timid," he wrote in a memorandum to the board, "but I am convinced that such a program can be accomplished and that without it we can reconcile ourselves to the strategy of our existing situation: pockets of excellence and sinks of despair floating in a slough of despond. . . . We increasingly discern the need to do more than fine tune our existing programs."

Mr. Sobol went so far as to recommend the imposition of a state mandated plan and removal of the local board of education in cases of failing schools. The issue of what comprises a failing school was not discussed, but it seems logical that schools have failed when there is no improvement in student achievement after a year of schooling.

Mr. Sobol proposed that schools which do not produce learning outcomes be "de-registered" and the parents of such schools be given vouchers to permit their children to attend nonpublic schools. While a number of states are debating the issue of evaluating schools and districts on the basis of school outcomes, Mr. Sobol has advocated bold initiatives.

Put simply, a results oriented package is used to evaluate schools on the basis of whether student achievement is improving rather than whether they meet state regulations. The linchpin of a results oriented package plan is student outcomes. Results will be the bases for determining the caliber of the school board, superintendent, principal, and teachers.

Mr. Sobol's plan, as well as the guaranteed achievement package suggested in this chapter, allows school administrators wide latitude to choose the teachers with whom they will work. This puts the teachers' unions in an adversarial position, but since unions are a large part of the cause of the decline in learning, their opposition should be disregarded.

Governor Tommy G. Thompson of Wisconsin has been more effective in dealing with teachers' unions than anyone else. In his words,

> I'm willing to take on the teachers' unions and drag them kicking and screaming into the 20th century. If I am re-elected, I will drag them into the 21st century (*Education Week* 10/31/90).

In England, where reform is well on its way, teachers' unions have established "escape committees." This action was initiated to find a way out for teachers who feel uncomfortable with change or those who do not feel they could be productive in the new system. The function of the "escape committees" is to help these teachers find other jobs.

The area where the teachers' union is having the most devastating effect is the insistence on the preservation of tenure (lifetime jobs). This job security concept is especially disastrous in states like New Jersey where superintendents and principals are also given tenure after three years of employment. The average cost of dismissing an incompetent educator who has been given tenure is $70,000. If schools are to improve, a way must be found to quickly get rid of incompetent educators. The easiest solution is for states to abolish the practice of giving tenure.

In summary, the education reform movement which has been led by the states is in its eighth year and counting. Leaders in policy making are beginning to realize that throwing money at the problems of education has not and will not make a difference. The new emphasis must be on system change and making the systems' personnel accountable.

The idea of schools guaranteeing achievement is an idea which needs to be put on a fast track. It will give the reform movement the momentum which it has lacked. The best advice one can give to state policy leaders is to "stand firm; don't flinch." The pressure from the establishment against this major reform is going to be enormous.

A STATE OF DETERMINATION: THE CONNECTICUT PLAN

In 1983 when *A Nation At Risk* reported,

> the educational foundations of our society are presently being eroded by a rising tide of mediocrity,

all fifty states responded with some type of program for educational reform. Almost universally, these reforms were aimed at secondary education. The major premise of this book is that until America awakens to the realization that school improvement must focus on the earlier years of learning, there will be no real gains in learning outcomes.

While all of the states have initiated some type of educational reform, the most determined effort has been made in Connecticut (*Wall Street Journal* 4/24/90). Reform efforts there have focused on two issues: (1) where are the schools failing? (2) what will it take to bring them up to snuff?

The Connecticut plan has blazed a trail that politicians from President Bush down and educators across the country are starting to follow in the national effort to improve education. The heart of the plan is to (1) set goals, (2) test for how well they are being reached, (3) hold educators responsible for their being achieved.

While all of the states except North Dakota have accountability systems, most plans are either pusillanimous or generally not working, because they fail to hold individual educators responsible when there is a lack of learning. The approach to accountability in most states is to hold the school or the school system accountable instead of educators. Schools and school districts are intangible objects not subject to answerability in the true meaning of the word. Accountability must be expected from individuals, not institutions.

Unlike any other state, Connecticut holds individual educators responsible for learning deficits and its system of tests is designed to pinpoint whether deficiencies are in the curriculum, leadership, or instruction.

The Connecticut plan tests all fourth, sixth, and eighth graders in the "Three R's," reading, writing, and arithmetic. Central to the examination is a forty-five minute writing exercise. Multiple choice tests in math measure computation and problem solving skills along with the ability to interpret data from graphs. A reading test measures comprehension and the ability to draw inferences.

Each December, parents and school officials get detailed scores on the performance of each child. In January, school district reports are published on the front page of every newspaper in the state, and if a superintendent wants to keep his job, he had better make certain that his schools do well.

The net result of the Connecticut plan is to make school officials individually accountable for the progress of students. The outcomes of the published tests amount to "a public report card." This makes it possible for parents and voters to assess how their schools compare with others in the state. A significant outcome of the tests has been to demonstrate to teachers that they have not been doing the job and to help them improve their teaching.

The Connecticut plan provides each superintendent with an analysis of the scores of his district. The superintendent can then decide what action is needed. Perhaps the best feature of the Connecticut tests is that they pinpoint students who need extra help. Further, the state requires that extra help be given to students who fall below a certain level.

As part of the state's education improvement drive, local schools have eliminated some recess time, reduced movement time from one room to another, and generally added as much as forty-five minutes a day to time available for teaching. Principals have been given more authority over their teaching staffs and the instructional programs. Most importantly, they are held accountable when students in the school they administer fail to learn.

Teachers are required to closely check homework performance, and students who fall behind must stay after school or return on Saturday mornings. School districts throughout the state have begun urging the parents of children younger than ten (in the fourth grade or below) to read to their children for at least ten minutes every night.

Two outcomes are that teachers are required to do a lot more work and the increased accountability places school managers under much greater stress. To compensate for these two happenings, Connecticut has increased the average teachers' salary 41 percent since 1986. The average is now $41,600 a year, considerably higher than the nation's $31,000.

Initially, many superintendents and school boards resisted the larger state role, but the state board of education persisted, and Connecticut is now regarded as having the best diagnostic tests in the country. The important thing is that the tests are administered at the fourth, sixth, and eighth grade levels, which are benchmark periods of growth in education. The action of the state reflects the realization that their students compete with students all over the world, not just other students within the state.

The Connecticut program is in stark contrast to programs in many other states which fail to hold individuals accountable but attempt to hold schools accountable. Many of these states give incentives to schools which perform well and apply sanctions against schools which do poorly. Both of these ideas are absurd. Why should schools be rewarded for doing what they are supposed to do in the first place, teach the student well? And the notion of applying sanctions against schools which are doing poorly is even more absurd. These schools need help, not penalties. The solution is to change inept teachers and principals.

At the heart of the Connecticut program is the requirement that school districts implement remedial programs starting in first grade to prevent students from falling behind. Every state should follow Connecticut's lead and require its school districts to implement support programs in the earliest years of education. Best results will be achieved if these programs are initiated starting in kindergarten. Other states should follow Connecticut's burgeoning trend to hold administrators responsible and accountable for learning.

THE SCHOOL DISTRICT REPORT CARD

Not only are schools and districts a long way from guaranteeing learning. Even the most caring parents and concerned taxpayers find it nearly impossible to learn how their school district measures up. In order to meet this issue head-on, several states have taken the unprecedented step of issuing annual report cards which assess the performance of school districts. The intent is to obtain a much higher level of public involvement by focusing public attention on the operation and outcomes of local education systems. The report cards compare each districts' taxes, spending, and academic achievement both with other districts and the state average.

The school district report card comprises an accurate profile of the education system in a particular school district. The focal point of districtwide report cards is to give taxpayers and parents a clear sense of school district policies, priorities, school budgets, and the performance of students.

The district report card includes such key fiscal data as the amount of state aid, local school tax rates, and the amount of increased spending over the previous years. It also embodies performance data of the district's students such as dropout rates, students' attendance, test results by schools, and the percentage of students continuing their education after high school. The selected indicators give insight into district spending, staffing patterns, and student performance. The card provides trend data and comparison figures from other districts. This focuses public attention on both the quality and the efficiency of the schools in the district.

The state department of education would send copies of district report cards to every newspaper in the state, libraries, and civic organizations. School districts would be requested to distribute them to parents and taxpayers.

Following is a selected list of items included on a school district's report card. The card also reports data from other districts in order that taxpayers and parents can see how their district compares to similar districts and the state average.

Amount the district pays its teachers

Attendance rate of students

Percentage of students passing the proficiency tests

S.A.T. scores and the results of Advanced Placement Examinations

Percentage of students with special needs

Percentage of ninth graders graduating three years later

Percentage of graduates continuing their education

Percentage of students changing schools

District per pupil expenditure

Hours schools are in session

Ratio of professional staff to students

Students' performance in reading, mathematics and science

Expenditures per pupil

While the school district report cards rankle school boards and superintendents to whom they often are an embarrassment, parents and taxpayers consider them among the most imaginative and productive of state policies. Alibis and excuses from educators are inappropriate since the report cards show a comparison of each district contrasted with every other district and the state average.

The practice of issuing school district report cards by governor's offices and state departments of education is expected to spread. Similar action will undoubtedly become standard operating procedure in most states in spite of strong objections from teachers' unions, school board members and superintendents. What will be the outcomes of district report cards? It is too early to tell but the effect will certainly be traumatic. In late 1990 the state of New Jersey released the most comprehensive and informative district report card yet developed. The New Jersey Association of School Administrators issued a press release charging the governor's office and state department of education with "education bashing." The public subsequently rejected 44 percent of the states' school districts' budgets. Whatever the eventual outcomes of annual detailed reports to the public, the public has the right to know and become involved. They also are entitled to know how their district compares with others. Furthermore, the reports are an important instrument in the move towards guaranteed learning.

ON THE BRINK OF REFORM

The fifty state governors are approaching clean-cut and stringent school reform as is evidenced in their statement following a meeting in late 1989, "Our public education system must be fundamentally restructured in order to assure that all students meet higher standards" (National Governors Assn. Minutes 1989). They called for a new focus on results over procedures; provision for "gifted professionals" to teach without education degrees; and more say for parents in where children go to school and how the schools are run. While they are nearing a demand for school districts to produce results, they have not yet taken this final step. Simply announcing that schools should produce results is too tame a response to the crisis.

It is extremely difficult to get educators to admit that more of the same will not be good enough. When they are asked to change what they have been doing, it makes them feel like bad people who have failed. This points to the inescapable conclusion that the schools cannot be enticed or cajoled into reform.

They must be directed to do so and the jobs of the administrative and teaching force put on the line if positive results do not follow.

States are beginning to target the nature and quality of school administration and are expected to make the elementary principalship the flagship of the school reform movement. It is anticipated that nearly 40 percent of current elementary principals will leave their jobs over the next five years, opening a demographic window to influence the improvement of learning. This affords an unusual opportunity to concentrate on the employment of large numbers of women and minorities; but the overriding consideration in employing principals must be a high degree of intelligence.

It is time for the fifty governors to go beyond goals, as important as they are. The time for action is at hand. The message to educators running schools should be an ultimatum to reform and produce outcomes or move on and let someone be appointed who can. Just as companies depend upon the caliber of their workforce, schools depend upon the quality, intellectual performance, and creativity of the individuals who staff the schools. This premise is the major drive initiating reform. All other inferences and presuppositions are subordinate and should be treated as such. Navigating around the mine fields of education includes sweeping away incompetent principals, inept teachers, and balky custodians.

STATE INTERVENTION

State intervention should take place when school districts fail to improve after consistently poor performance of students. Any district with schools where students have unacceptably low standardized reading and mathematics scores and fail to improve after three years should be taken over by the state and operated under the authority of the commissioner of education. School board members should be dismissed and a superintendent reporting direct to the commissioner installed with special powers to oust ineffective principals and teachers and to implement changes in curriculum and instruction. Takeover of a district with failing schools negates all agreements which the school board made with a teacher's union in order that the intervention will not be hampered in its efforts towards rapid improvement.

A NEED TO BOOST MOTIVATION

In the search for ways to boost excessively low levels of school achievement, educators need to examine the root causes of the lack of student motivation.

Society is sending a message that students need only do as little as it takes to get by. All elements of society should send a new signal to students letting them know that success in school is directly connected to success in life. Business and industry on their part must tie reading skills to employment. And the schools themselves must demand more of students and at the same time stop presenting material in a boring fashion that deadens their interest in learning.

Currently, students do not work very hard in school. They must be brought to an understanding of the strong link between effort and performance. The schools' initiative to boost motivation must center around a more demanding curriculum beginning in the primary school and continuing throughout the intermediate years.

CHAPTER 7

Significant Issues in Improving Student Outcomes

Elementary school educators have contributed heavily to the nation's educational drag, but the broader American society must accept the responsibility for passively supporting and tolerating a system of schools that is now among the worst in the civilized world. For too long the emphasis on school improvement has been on "input" in education. Finally, the shift from "input" to "output" has become an accelerating trend.

If the schools are to improve dramatically and increase their productivity, a number of sensitive issues must be addressed with candor. Critical among these matters are the issues of testing and improved education for minorities. Schools have failed miserably to accomplish their mission in these areas or to even address them openly.

TESTING: A MISSION IN DISREPAIR

Standardized testing in America's elementary schools is in a serious state of intellectual disrepair. A West Virginia physician blew the whistle on this activity in 1987 when he conducted a private survey and found that all fifty states claimed to be above average in school achievement. His investigation, which revealed education fraud being perpetrated on the public, has had a leveling effect, but more is needed.

While there are a number of reasons for the absurdity of the claim that every state is above average, a major cause is the lack of security of test items, particularly in the elementary schools where principals allow teachers to administer standardized tests to their own pupils. Another problem is the practice in elementary schools of using commercial tests, many of which are out of date, and all of which make excessive use of the multiple choice format. In the words of Chester Finn, chairman of the National Assessment Governing Board,

> We have relied on a motley array of commercial tests and state assessment programs. Sloppiness and cheating are rampant. . . . It's staggering, given the vast amount of testing in our schools, that no governor can tell how the reading and mathematics skills, or science and history knowledge of youngsters in his state stack up alongside those in other jurisdictions (*Education Week* 2/7/90).

Because school administrators have not created a reliable system of measuring achievement, the results they achieve are subject to the whims and the profiteering motives of commercial test makers. The outcome is, when states compile all of the local school district scores, nobody is below average.

In brief there are currently available no dependable measures of student learning that are consistent from school to school, district to district, and state to state. Yet, the ability of a superintendent to improve schools in his district depends upon his knowledge of his students' achievement as it compares with the achievement of other students in similar school districts and the state as a whole.

In spite of the compelling need for quality national measures of achievement, the nation's leading organizations of educators vigorously oppose plans to broaden the mission of the National Assessment of Educational Progress (the nation's report card). Proposals in the Congress to expand this reliable operation to allow state by state, district by district, and school by school comparisons have incurred the wrath of the national superintendents' association, the national curriculum organization, the national organizations of both high school and elementary principals as well as both national teachers' unions. It is disappointing, but perhaps not surprising, that these vested interest organizations have petitioned President Bush to veto legislation which will allow an expanded National Assessment to make state, district, and school comparisons.

Just why are the nation's school administrator and teacher groups objecting to this sound educational proposal? One can only conjecture that they are fearful that the public will learn the real truth about how poorly the nation's students are performing and how little is actually being learned in school. Educators are apparently more comfortable with the present practice in which (1) they select tests to be used in their individual school districts and (2) the tests are administered under their supervision. As long as this deplorable situation exits, the public must continue to rely on inferior indicators which administrators manipulate as the national gauge of educational effectiveness.

Fortunately, the Chief State School Officers Organization of the fifty states, allied with the fifty governors, is committed to establishing and attaining national performance standards. They support the expanded assessment. Hopefully, the clout of these two groups will prevail over the lobbying of the president by the national associations of various educational groups which so rigorously and unreasonably oppose national standards.

In an age of international economic competition, it is essential that the educational product of our schools be determined by the best possible measures. It is also imperative that students be assessed by tests of recognized quality, developed by the nation's leading psychometricians, rather than profit-oriented commercial companies.

Despite the opposition from educators, a long overdue national testing system containing a set of measures which each child should master at a certain level is in the offing. The National Education Goals panel which was set up by the president to monitor progress towards education goals is in the process of developing a new national assessment system. The purpose is to create a situation where every child has an opportunity to take an achievement test and know where he is, and parents can know where their children are. The results of the tests will also be used as a part of the national report card which will be issued annually to inform citizens on the status of the schools.

LIABILITY OF MINORITY TEACHERS AS ROLE MODELS

Recent research at Harvard on why black and Hispanic students in predominantly minority school districts fail to learn has opened Pandora's box. Harvard University's Ronald Ferguson told the Northeast Midwest Congressional Coalition that the cause was poor teaching. He reported that teachers in minority districts consistently score lower on state competency tests than do teachers in largely white districts. (*Challenge: A Journal of Research on Black Men* 1991)

The researcher divulged incontestable findings which conclude that teacher performance is a significant factor in keeping students in poverty. A soon to be published study headed by Professor Ferguson reveals that, "Teachers test score differentials are among the important differences in why minority children do so poorly when compared to non-minority children." He and other experts contend that without quality teachers, minority students will not achieve.

Unfortunately, Ferguson declined to reveal test score differences between teachers in predominantly minority districts and predominantly white districts. It is this kind of timidity, when it comes to facing up to minority deficiencies, which prohibits our coping with the inability of minority children to learn in elementary school. Key educators nationwide are more concerned about not rocking the boat and pandering to demands of civil rights groups than getting a handle on the minority learning problem. Civil rights groups and the courts erroneously insist that minority children be assigned minority teachers as role models; school administrators, who should know better, meekly comply. In cooperating with this delusive reasoning, the poorest teachers are alloted to children who need to improve their learning the most. If assigning teachers as role models is incompatible with quality learning outcomes, then the role model notion should be abandoned.

What is now clear is that the education of minority children will not improve until the quality of their teaching improves. This cannot happen while the malpractice of allocating minority teachers to minority students prevails. Minority children need and deserve our best teachers.

Contributing heavily to the inadequacy of minority teachers is the absence of quality in their education and teacher training. A very high percentage of minority individuals who earn teaching certificates graduate from historically black colleges and universities. For example, in Florida, the proportion of blacks who enter teaching from a black college or university is 50 percent. These colleges have long been underfunded, and while progress is being made they need substantial additional resources.

The distinguished scholar Jacques Barzun expressed grave concern about the practice of assigning minority teachers to minority children when he wrote:

> As for the notion that black children can learn only from black teachers and about black things, that is very dangerous because it really means that racism is in the ascendancy and that we're all going to be living in groups of haggling, competing, name calling separatists (*Education Week* 10/27/90).

The education of minority children will not improve dramatically until the quality of their teaching improves, and this cannot happen as long as the practice of designating minority teachers to minority students is demanded by civil rights groups, ordered by the courts, and truckled to by school superintendents and principals.

MINORITY LEARNING IN THE EARLY GRADES

A widely recognized phenomenon is the evidence that minority children are not achieving in the nation's elementary schools. If minorities are allowed to continue to exhibit substantially lower levels of literacy attainment than non minorities, this will present substantial problems for the military, industry, and society at large. Evidence clearly shows that undesirable outcomes are associated with low levels of literacy and mathematical attainment, e.g., increased crime rates and unemployment along with an inability to adapt to the continual change of society.

The data requires that a massive effort be made to improve

learning outcomes for minority children in the earliest grades. Although this is the area of schooling where society gets the most bang for the buck, paradoxically it spends less per pupil than any other part of schooling. To accomplish this task, it may become necessary to have no class with more than fifteen students; but if that is what it takes, then we must be about it. We simply cannot tolerate having children not learning in school. Whatever resources are needed to educate minority children well in early grades should be shifted from the top-heavy college and university level where highest expenditures per students are currently allocated.

When minority children are helped to achieve well in the primary grades, not only will they live richer lives, but many of society's most insidious problems will be eased. Education is not just a means to make a living; it also makes for a liveable world.

MAGNET ELEMENTARY SCHOOLS

A magnet school is best defined as a school with an expanded attendance boundary in which there are program offerings and facilities that focus on particular areas of merit. The student population is racially heterogeneous.

The magnet school movement, which was first initiated as a secondary school innovation in inner cities, has recently become a part of the elementary school reform movement. The magnet elementary school idea is spreading rapidly to the nation's more perceptive school districts which have difficulty mixing racial groups. Magnets are by far the most effective tools we know of for improving the quality of education while balancing racial and ethnic ratios.

Magnet schools comprise islands of choice within a traditional school district assignment plan. The school staff selects a particular educational theme as the school's main focus. The theme chosen is one which is appealing to the group of students it wants to attract. Examples of areas of concentration are the use of Montessori instruction, or a focus on the arts or sciences. Magnets have open enrollment policies for a limited number of students throughout the district who share similar interests.

Magnets serve a racially mixed population by offering unique educational programs to which transportation is provided in order to make out-of-the-ordinary educational experiences available to students beyond the boundaries of a single attendance zone.

A number of types of elementary magnet schools are now functioning throughout the country. While no hard evaluative data is available, since the schools have been in existence only from two to three years, staff, parents and students reflect an increase in support and enthusiasm for schooling.

Magnet schools are keyed to the need to attract students of similar interests but diverse ethnicities into a learning environment where each child can advance. Features of magnetism include special subject focus, area focus, special teaching strategies, unique programing, extensive use of technology, and extended day activity.

While magnet schools hold special promise for improving the quality of education of the black poor, who are geographically and socially isolated, they perform a variety of other functions. Their potential for diverse organization to deal with a particular sector of school population is well demonstrated in the models already established by a few of the nation's school districts.

Elementary magnet schools are highly recommended as a technique for improving the quality of elementary education while balancing racial and ethnic ratios. They do this by selecting a school in the center of an all-black residential area. The intent is to make programs in these schools so appealing that they will attract students from other residential areas.

An underlying premise is that magnet schools with strong programs will attract private school and suburban students on a voluntary basis. Substantial suburban participation in urban schools is essential to address the decline of the white population in urban areas. For this reason the magnet school idea is becoming increasingly popular as a leading innovation in the elementary school reform movement.

Magnets are characterized by five elements: (1) theme-based curriculum, (2) role in desegregation, (3) voluntary enrollment, (4) access to students beyond regular school boundaries, (5) quality education for minorities.

TYPES OF MAGNET ELEMENTARY SCHOOLS

Each school which undertakes the mission of becoming a magnet school develops a statement of purpose that outlines its distinctive features and arranges for families to be involved in sorting out the parameters of its curriculum. The following areas of focus have proven successful in magnet elementary schools.

Classical Academy with Uniforms

The program of the classical academy is offered within an environment in which students and staff wear uniforms. High standards of student behavior and regular attendance are required. The program concentrates on excellence in reading with an emphasis on reading and mathematics. All literature used for reading is classical. Other offerings which are emphasized are writing and music. Many magnet schools have found requiring students to wear uniforms vastly improves the school climate.

Individually Guided Education

The objective of the IGE magnet is to provide instruction based on each student's particular needs and learning style. Students are deployed into multi-age groups rather than by conventional grade level groupings. The mission of this program is to guide students in their individual development. The curriculum is designed to assist students in self-directed learning.

Environmental Science/Museum Studies

The mission of the environmental science magnet is to provide students an opportunity to learn certain scientific skills including observing, classifying, measuring, and interpreting evidence through hands-on experiences. All science is firsthand and combines classroom experiences with museum visits, day camps, field trips, lab demonstrations, environmental programs, and outside speakers.

International Studies

The international studies magnet provides students the opportunity to develop, explore, and expand their understanding of different peoples, languages, and cultures. Geography is emphasized as a separate subject. Study of a second language is required.

Montessori

The Montessori magnet stresses teacher respect for the growing child. Teachers are trained to recognize when and how each child needs to be taught. Montessori methods of instruction and materials allow children to learn by self-discovery at an individually determined pace. The classroom reflects an environment of concentration, independence, problem solving, and competency in academic skills.

Visual and Performing Arts

The visual and performing arts magnet offers children in K–6 a well-rounded program in art, music, drama, dance. While these are peripheral subjects, the school's focus on reading and mathematics is the central core of the curriculum. Performance opportunities are available for all children at all levels on a regular basis.

SCHOOL BASED CHILD CARE

Demographic data on changing family lifestyles makes the establishment of massive programs in school based child care inevitable. With 45.3 percent of young children living in homes with both parents working and 22.4 percent living with a single parent, it is politically expedient that the burden on these parents be eased in a magnitude not seen before in America.

All disadvantaged and disabled children must have access to high quality preschool programs by the age of three. The caliber of early child care and education must be greatly strengthened and coordinated with kindergarten learning. It is essential that all children be prepared for entering kindergarten and that kindergarten is prepared for them.

Currently 56 percent of women with children under age six are in the work force, which means that many parents are forced to make choices they should not have to make, and young children are exposed to the potentially damaging effects of poor quality care. This calls for major changes in the national child care system, which must focus on a shortage of high quality child care for infants and small children.

The most promising solution is for high quality child care programs to be school based. They should be established at and operated by the nation's elementary schools.

An ideal system of schooling will first engage economically poor students at age three. The target group is students who are commonly referred to as being at-risk. Schools can and should offer a rich learning environment for those children who are already showing signs of cultural starvation.

While private providers of child care should be encouraged to expand and develop programs of high quality, an established institution like the school is best prepared to serve as the hub for child care programs for three- and four-year-olds.

The major benefit to society of a commitment to quality early child care is its effect in stemming later school failure and delinquency. Data indicates that about the same number of kindergarteners are deficient in school readiness skills as dropped out of school in the 1989–90 school year. Once elementary schools begin to serve as centers and offer quality early child care, an outcome is curricular continuity between the preschool program which emphasizes hands-on play-oriented learning, and kindergartens. If the nation really believes that children who are successful in school make successful citizens, and the research overwhelmingly concludes that it does, then school based child care becomes a new imperative for the country's elementary schools.

PARENT INVOLVEMENT

Parents are the first and most powerful teachers of children. If they are knowledgeable about supporting their children's early learning, they can powerfully influence school readiness. The establishment of strong relationships between parents and children in the early months of life has been shown to have significant implications for children's later development. And these relationships are more likely to develop when parents have time and the emotional energy to interact with their young children.

Parents who are not equipped to support their children's early learning must be trained to do so. Parent education which teaches new parents how to create a home learning environment must be expanded to include all low income mothers.

American homes must be places of learning where parents play an active role in their children's early learning, particularly by reading to them on a daily basis. Poor and undereducated parents should have access to the support and training required to fulfill this role.

ACADEMIC CONTESTS

An encouraging new intellectual activity in elementary schools is the growing number of schools participating in academic competition. Involvement in classroom quiz programs is becoming part of the regular curriculum in many elementary schools beginning as early as kindergarten.

The boom in academic competition is a response to demands for improving the quality of elementary education nationwide. Student involvement in academic contests is multiplying fast and the outcomes are encouraging. For example, when the National Geographic Society started a geography bee for elementary grades four to eight, it anticipated that several thousand schools would participate. More than 32,000 schools signed up.

Many educators are convinced that the excitement of participating in academic contests promotes teamwork and spurs a love of learning. As an added incentive, grants to schools and scholarships for students ride on the outcome of the national academic contest. With all the excitement about academic competition among students, teachers, and parents in participating schools, the movement was dismayed by a charge from the National Association of Secondary Principals that the intensive academic preparation for a ten event academic decathlon takes away time from other school work.

This is the same principals' organization which warned against the setting of national performance goals and lobbied Congress against allowing the National Assessment for Education Progress to report the outcomes of assessment which would compare schools and school districts.

What is so incongruous about the principals' objections is that many school principals are former coaches and consequently avid supporters of athletic contests. It is strange indeed that they would so adamantly and unreasonably oppose intellectual competition.

Fortunately, the National Association for Elementary School Principals has not joined in such a poorly thought through position. On the contrary, the elementary association is highly supportive.

CORPORATE AMERICA, THE NEW DILETTANTE

Roughly eight years ago, business and industry started dabbling in education. Much of the effort has revolved around buying computers or other equipment. While over 100,000 business-school partnerships have been formed since 1983, most of the initiatives from industry are "feel good" efforts which have had little impact on school improvement.

Corporate America's input has largely been limited to empty, "adopt a school," or partnership efforts where someone from the business partnership drops off a check with the principal for books, computers, or new band uniforms. A photographer from the local newspaper is usually present for the occasion and the outcome is that everyone has a happy feeling but there is no impact on learning.

A 1990 study by the Conference Board says corporate America must share the blame for the growing illiteracy rate because of its failure to test prospective employees for reading skills. The study identifies areas where weak reading skills have seriously hurt workplace performance. A number of the firms surveyed traced a variety of problems to illiteracy. The problems ranged from the inability of workers to read instructions resulting in machinery breakdowns, to clerks getting facts wrong on instructions and misfiling papers. Corporate America was also indicted by the Conference Board for failure to demand high school transcripts when evaluating applicants for employment. By not ascertaining reading skills and demanding transcripts, business is failing to support the outcomes of learning and sending the wrong signal to job applicants. Consequently, it is contributing directly to the wretched situation in which each succeeding high school class is less employable than its successor.

The epitome of the matter of business partnerships is that they are acquiring the dreary and depressing look of federally supported projects of the 1960s. They encourage schools to tinker, and schools are expert at makeshift practices. The outcome is that business money often goes to projects of little effect.

Perhaps the best evidence that corporations are woefully out of step with educational reform is seen in the 1990 grant of the Exxon Educational Foundation of $1.25 million to reform colleges of education. The grant to John Goodlad's Center for Educational Renewal at the University of Washington brings to $2.37 million the total invested in the project by Exxon. By Mr. Goodlad's own admission, it will require ten years to reform these outdated institutions which are no more than a ponderous drag on teaching and learning. Furthermore, the nation cannot wait for ten years to improve teacher education.

Corporations concerned about the quality of schooling must come to recognize that the area most in need of reform and most capable of giving the best return on the investment is the nation's primary and intermediate schools. If big business is really serious about school improvement, it needs more acumen about how and where to go about being of help to this arena of education.

CHAPTER 8

The Cause of the Decline in Learning

The parade of scathing reports documenting the ills of America's faltering school system has consistently failed to deal with the primary cause of the plunge in learning which began in the early 1960's and is still continuing. The customary indictment is directed at (1) lack of parental involvement (2) disruptive students (3) drugs. As incredible as it may seem, the problem that consistently gets kid-glove treatment is the lack of a quality teaching force. Yet this is the clue to improving schools.

Rather than pinpointing poor teaching as the culprit, education experts tiptoe around this issue and persist in elaborating on the complaints of disgruntled teachers. It is time to face the fact that obsession with the misery index of discontented teachers and the myriad suggestions that what they need is more money, more respect, and more power to make decisions, reflects a preposterous ignorance of the problem. The way schools are currently organized, teachers have more than enough power already, especially at the elementary level where their role includes being legislator, executive, and judiciary.

ONE HORN OF THE DILEMMA

Education experts have ignored the premise that if American schools had been staffed by a quality teaching force, the precipitous and shocking declines in achievement would never have occurred. Until the public confronts the issue that the absence of a preeminent teaching force is at the root of the problem, the best we can expect in student achievement is marginal improvement.

There is a growing body of evidence showing that the academic status of teachers is in deep decline relative to other professions. It is now apparent that the people who will soon be teaching in our schools are those with the least academic ability of all Americans attending college. The serious downtrend in the learning of high school students as measured by College Board Examinations is common knowledge, but the drop in the College Board scores of prospective teachers is astronomical.

When the academic achievement of all professions is compared, the quality of people coming into teaching is near the bottom, ranking only above African studies. The average College Board verbal score of prospective teachers is at a low of 391. To put this matter into perspective, the average S.A.T. verbal score of the nation's high school seniors is 424. Furthermore, teaching has become a haven for 24 percent of all white males who score in the lowest 20 percent on the College Board's verbal exam.

The dramatic slump in quality of candidates for teaching in the public schools is to a considerable extent a result of the womens' liberation movement. For many years, women were restricted in their career opportunities. Because of the absence of opportunities available to them, they were attracted to teaching, librarianship, and nursing. The quality of these women was usually very high, and they made a massive contribution to the quality of teaching. These women are the unsung heroes of American education, but they are gone and their replacements are unacceptably inferior.

Interesting insight into the inadequacy of the teaching force is contained in a survey of public school teachers (National Center for Education Survey 1990) in which 78 percent of teachers said they are very well prepared in subject matter knowledge. What happens to the unfortunate students being taught by a whopping 22 percent who, by their own admission, are unprepared in the subject matter they are teaching? It is folly to assume that students will learn when their teachers are ill-prepared. A mere 46 percent of the teaching force said they are well prepared in recognizing students' learning styles, and only 56 percent reported they are well prepared in understanding child and adolescent development.

The reason the teachers gave for being in teaching is another indicator causing serious concern about the caliber of the teaching force. For example, 32 percent mentioned job security, 31 percent cited long summer vacations, and 30 percent "have too much involved to leave now." These motives can hardly be called inspirational.

Teachers in poll after poll complain of being underpaid and undervalued. Yet their salaries have risen 77 percent since the 1980–81 school year. In 1990 the average teacher was paid $31,403 for 9.5 months of work.

What is there to show for the immense increase in teachers' salaries? Test scores continue to fall, dropout rates have increased dramatically, and teachers are more dissatisfied. Yet, prominent educators and teachers' unions are proposing that the road to reform is to "empower" teachers; somehow this will make them happy. A recent editorial entitled "Not Happy Teachers—Better Teachers" concludes that,

> A system that rewards mediocrity and incompetence and treats everyone alike whether they are any good or not is not going to produce high levels of competence (*Wall Street Journal* 10/26/90).

The country's inability to educate vast numbers of citizens is due largely to inept teachers. This situation is creating a social time bomb, but so far the politicians who control education at the state and local levels have lacked the moral and political will to defuse it.

Antiquated Education Laws

An urgent imperative is the need for states to overhaul their antiquated education laws protecting the jobs of teachers and cease giving them lifetime contracts. It is all but impossible for school systems to rid themselves of incompetent teachers; instead, they shuffle them from one location to another or promote them to the central office staff in order to get them out of the schools. Time is running out for governors and legislators to pass and implement legislation for dramatically changing laws which protect incompetence in schools.

An Albatross Around the Neck of Reform: Colleges of Education

A significant strategy for repairing elementary schools is to improve the quality of potential teachers coming into the system. At present, all elementary teachers are required to spend nearly half of their entire college careers in education courses with the result that most of them have practically no course work in mathematics and science, two of the most important subjects they are required to teach. This malpractice leads to the inescapable conclusion that colleges of education are not preparing teachers; they are training educationists. They are sort of fitting teachers for an unfitted fitness.

In its landmark report the National Commission on Excellence conducted a survey of 1,350 teacher training institutions and expressed alarm over the findings:

> Forty-one percent of the time of elementary school teacher candidates is spent in education courses, which reduces the amount of time available for subject matter courses. . . . Teacher preparation programs need substantial improvement (A Nation At Risk, 22).

Although the commission issued its report in 1983, instead of improving, the teacher training institutions have continued to plod along in pedestrian fashion, oblivious to increasing calls to do something about their deplorable operation.

The evidence of disarray in teacher training is too obvious to escape attention. The problems colleges of education create are substantial, much more serious and complex than is generally admitted. First and foremost is their calamitous effect on elementary education. This stranglehold has given rise to an episodic indictment of the institutions for not preparing teachers and administrators with clear ideas of educational relevance. In a profession that is so far behind the times, teacher training institutions are viewed by many as both self-serving and irresponsible. In addition to what some view as a perpetuation of antiquated teaching methodology, the abundance of pedagogy-oriented course work crowds out subject area learning, which is the most critical component of teacher effectiveness. Teacher certification, a widely acknowledged mess, must also be laid at the door of the colleges of education because of their vigorous lobbying of state departments of education for criteria which benefit only their graduates.

A point of view stubbornly espoused by many in colleges of education is that knowing how to teach is more important than knowing what to teach. This is a failed idea and one which largely accounts for the miserable state of mathematics and science education in the elementary schools. Their lack of familiarity with contemporary learning theories and state of the art applications of technology also contribute to the public perception that teacher training institutions are more related to the problems in education than the solution.

In a recent hearing conducted by the governor's office in Florida on the performance of colleges of education, (Florida Commission on School Reform 1989) every presenter who gave testimony made harsh criticisms of the institutions. While some of the criticism was general in nature, representatives from the Department of Education pinpointed the fact that the teacher training schools have failed miserably to prepare beginning teachers in the use of educational technology.

In late 1990 John Goodlad, education researcher and president of the American Association of Colleges for Teacher Education, published a grim report on the condition of teacher education. Although Goodlad himself has had a long career as a college of education professor, he pulled no punches in his criticism. His findings revealed an enterprise suffering from unstable leadership, low status, an unclear mission, and a narrow view of teaching. After studying twenty-nine teachers' training institutions in depth, his research lays out elaborate plans for reforming these moss back institutions. He suggested that at least ten years will be required to carry out the reform agenda.

This is educational nonsense. The urgency for improving schools is so critical that the nation cannot delay reforming any component of schooling for even a few months, much less for ten years. Furthermore, Goodlad's research, which deals with the abysmal state of teacher training, fails to address the most critical problem confronting the nation. The pool of college of education students currently training to be teachers are the lowest achievers in the nation's colleges and universities. A major factor is the lack of standards for admission to teacher training. In the 1,300 schools of education, admission standards to teacher training are so low that warm bodies, even lukewarm bodies, gain admission. The highest priority of the nation is to procure a source of teachers who are academically talented rather than continue with the low achieving graduates of the nation's colleges of education.

The solution to the problem is to abandon the colleges of education and allow local school districts to hire bright college graduates and train them in the schools where they are to teach. Society has for too long been patient and tolerant of our failed teacher training institutions.

Education's new national board of certification, which will begin certifying teachers who have excelled on a national basis in 1993, bypassed colleges of education when it resolved that education courses will not be a prerequisite to certification. The new certification policy was described editorially as follows:

> There is no need to have passed specific education courses or to be licensed by a state (*New York Times* 10/6/90).

What do prospective teachers study in the colleges of education? The typical program offers a smattering of education psychology, a bit of education history, a course in education philosophy, and a whole range of courses in methods of teaching.

J. Myron Atkin, writing as dean of the College of Education at Stanford, summed up the status of pedagogy as follows:

> It must be said that teaching is not an occupation with a firm and agreed upon large knowledge base from which the practitioner can draw to address problems that arise in a classroom. Neither is there a well-developed technology associated with high-school teaching nor an accompanying set of replicable skills that teachers transmit one to the other or that they learn during their program of preparation. At least, there is not as much of such

knowledge as is sometimes assumed to exist or that those who educate teachers often imply (Daedalus 1981).

The major obstacle to a higher caliber teaching force is the influence of colleges of education. Their unholy alliance with the states' departments of education deters entry into the teaching profession by requiring up to fifty semester hours of methods courses for a teaching credential. The end result is a frightful trifling with the lives of our children and youth.

State legislators should eliminate methods courses and realign the colleges of education as departments in the colleges of liberal arts. The only education courses worth salvaging are child development and adolescent psychology. Teaching methods on which current educational practice is based have been poorly tested and are ultimately divisive.

THE OTHER HORN OF THE DILEMMA

The poor quality of the teaching force is also responsible for the absence of quality in administration, since administrators are selected exclusively from the ranks of the teaching force. New Jersey is the only state to pass legislation permitting the selection of school managers from outside the teaching profession. Unfortunately, the establishment (superintendents), all of whom are college of education trained educators, have failed to take advantage of this enlightened legislation which sanctions the placement of bright and talented individuals from outside the profession in school management positions. The superintendents continue to hire school managers from the teaching corps.

Indication of a new trend is seen in action by the Milwaukee school board which recently sought and obtained new legislation to employ a superintendent from outside the profession and one with no previous experience in pre-collegiate education to be superintendent of the city's 98,000 student school district. The Wisconsin legislature quickly passed a special law permitting this action and the district followed through and hired a superintendent from outside the profession. This is believed to mark the first time in history that a major urban school district has engaged a non educator as its chief executive.

The action needed is so indisputable that it is impossible to understand why the states and school district leaders have failed to try corporate styles of management where the schools' managers have the power and responsibility of a CEO. There is no reason why the schools cannot be as well run as IBM, except for the absence of quality in leadership and on the teaching staff. When the school is directed by a CEO and reading and math scores do not go up, the CEO should be out at the end of his contract. The same criteria must be applied to teachers on his staff, who must be accountable for the educational outcomes in the classrooms of the schools where they work.

The issues of marginal teaching must become a top priority for school managers who work to meet the demands of today's world of education. No school can afford poor teaching by anyone. The marginal teachers who drift in and out of schools every day causing frustration among students must be identified and dismissed. At first blush this action may seem harsh, but when one considers what is happening to the nation's children, it is justifiable and overdue action.

In summary, the need for a higher caliber teaching force is critical. The matter urgently requires compelling action by the states' legislators and governors. Early action on this issue is imperative if the nation's public schools are to survive.

PERFORMANCE CONTRACTS FOR EDUCATORS

Employment contracts for school personnel as presently written are slanted towards assuring job security for educators. New contracts basing employment on student outcomes must replace these obsolete instruments. For administrators, the reformed contracts must focus on improvement in student achievement, school attendance, and parental involvement. The key words "achievement" and "student outcomes" must dominate the wording of agreements employing administrators.

Because of the new emphasis on accountability, school managers will face greater stress, but they are currently paid well without any specific responsibility beyond a general understanding that they will run the schools to the best of their ability. The problem with current contracts is that there is no clear sense of the results being sought. Once expected student outcomes are put in writing, and continued employment based upon their achievement, a world of difference will be seen in the schools.

In the case of teachers, the centerpiece of their contracts must be the measurable achievement of students; however, such matters as marking and returning homework and in-class writing assignments should also be specified and prescribed. Too many teachers assign busywork activities in class and homework which is never corrected and returned to the child. Children deserve to have all work marked and returned within two to three days. This factor alone will greatly increase the interest of children in their written assignments, especially homework. Having regular assessments made of their learning will keep children abreast of their progress and increase their motivation.

Teachers should be properly compensated for the extra time involved in correcting and returning papers. Furthermore, school boards should require children who fail to turn in their homework to attend classes on Saturday morning.

The problem with school reform is that it has not been very focused. People are fed up with the poor performance of educators. New contracts basing employment on student outcomes must replace the current obsolete instruments. For administrators, the reformed contracts must focus on improvement in student achievement, school attendance, and parental involvement.

A nationwide move to obtain higher quality teachers and give teachers high pay for high performance is a major step in the direction of turning around the school system.

CHAPTER 9

The Case for Curricular Reform in Elementary Schools

The cascade of studies dealing with the quality of the nation's schools has made it abundantly clear that by world norms, U.S. education is failing the nation. This fact alone makes the reform of education in science, mathematics, and technology a national priority. But there are other parameters also of great concern. The schools have simply not acted decisively in preparing minority children, on whom the nation's future must depend, for a world that changes radically in response to the mushrooming knowledge about science and technology.

Specific problems with education in the nation revolve around low test scores, student disinterest in science and mathematics, a demoralized and weakening teaching staff, low learning expectations, and a ranking at the bottom in international studies of science and mathematics education. All reports point to an alarming number of educational deficiencies and a growing crisis in American education.

The implications are a weakening of our scientific and technological preeminence in relation to other countries and a growing economic decline. These factors have already energized a set of disturbing economic and educational trends.

Beginning in 1980 the various states began legislating higher standards and stronger science and mathematics curricula for the high schools, but the elementary schools have been virtually ignored in the rush to implement reforms. Public policy has been searching for a "quick fix" by attempting to reform secondary education with little or no attention to elementary schools. Quick fixes always fail in education, and for understandable reasons. The most obvious of these is the mammoth size of the enterprise. The education of fifty million students located in eighty thousand schools distributed among fifty states simply cannot be easily or quickly changed. The solution requires determination, leadership, daring, and experimentation. This means that significant improvement will require more than just a year or two.

Our education system has its strong points, but a capacity for rapid change is not one of them. The various reports on the state of education have had some impact, but they have not improved learning. Their effect has been to underscore the strong connection which must exist between how well a nation can perform and the existence of high quality education. They have convinced the business sector of America that all children must be better educated in science, mathematics, and technology. Piecemeal reform will not get us out of our dilemma. Reform efforts must include all grades, all subject domains, and the length of time students spend in school.

THE PURPOSE OF CURRICULA REFORM

Curricula reforms in the elementary school should be aimed at (1) programs which will assure that all students are ready to start school, (2) programs which will assure that students continue to learn and master the reading and math skills taught in primary school, (3) students progress through the intermediate grades at their best pace but achieve at or above grade level.

READING: THE MOST IMPORTANT SUBJECT
IN THE ELEMENTARY SCHOOL

Reports released by the National Assessment of Educational Progress consistently indicate that students in the na-

The Case for Curricular Reform in Elementary Schools

tion's elementary schools spend little time on reading either in or out of school.

The assessment staff reported that very few fourth grade teachers (the level researched) used methods which will foster in-depth understanding of texts, such as having discussions in small groups or having children write about what they read. Teachers' emphasis is heavily weighted towards having students do workbook and skill-sheet excercises. This "busywork" approach has long been associated with poor teaching (*Education Week* 1/17/90).

NAEP reading research confirmed again in 1990 that black students, especially, continue to suffer from poor teaching. Black twelfth graders barely outperform white fourth graders in reading.

The report underscored the fact that children who read outside of class achieve significantly higher reading proficiency than those who do not. Confirmed also was the widely held impression that reading attainment is related to the amount of homework and classroom reading students perform.

Reading is the cornerstone of a child's success in school and life. While the nation receives a good return on the investment in education at all levels, research concludes that the return is highest from the primary school, which is the main delivery system for basic education and where children are first learning to read. Yet, paradoxically, this is the least costly of all levels of education.

It is incredible that educators have such little knowledge about how to teach reading. About the only thing they agree upon is that there is no best way. With this bald fact staring us in the face, it behooves parents to take a more active role in assuring that their children learn to read with proficiency.

Parents should tutor preschool children in the elements of reading. They can do this through opportunities that arise informally as part of everyday activities. An example of informal reading instruction is pointing out letters on signs while taking a walk or riding in a car. In the home, informal instruction also works very well when parents read to their children nightly before bedtime.

For parents who wish to teach their children to read at an

early age, (most children are ready to learn before they enter school), there are definite steps to follow. Children should start learning at the bottom of the reading ladder, first identifying letters, then working up through words and sentences to higher levels until they understand the meaning of the text. Once children are in school, parents' expectations, home language, and daily experience continue to influence how much and how well they read.

Research data (Becoming A Nation of Readers 1985) suggests an average third grader can read an unfamiliar story at the rate of one hundred words per minute. Poor readers at the third grade level can read the same story at fifty to seventy words per minute. Scholars contend the latter rate is so slow that it interferes with comprehension.

The quality of reading instruction in primary school has a profound impact on how well and how quickly children learn to read. Children taught by teachers who maintain high levels of motivation and conduct fast paced levels of instruction make larger than average gains on reading achievement test than do children taught by teachers who do otherwise.

Parents should read aloud to their children daily. Most parents do this at bedtime by reading a bedtime story. Both parents should engage in this practice by taking turns as a technique for impressing on children the importance of reading.

A survey conducted by a program of the Smithsonian Institution found that the top five favorite classic stories for bedtime reading are *Goldilocks and the Three Bears*, *Three Little Pigs*, *Cinderella*, *Snow White and the Seven Dwarfs*, and *The Wizard of Oz* (Reading is Fundamental 1989). Children's books are appropriate but parents should not stop there. Other important experiences include (1) reading aloud a favorite comic strip every day (2) reading aloud postcards and greeting cards that come in the mail (3) reading with the child the shopping list before trips to the grocery store. The intent is to assure that children understand at a very early age that the written word is important in all forms.

A major hindrance to the teaching of reading has been inadvertently created by the various state legislatures which require that a long list of social issues be taught beginning with kindergarten. This is done at the expense of teaching about reading and mathematics. While each state has its own pet docket of social matters, perhaps the worst offender is Florida, which does not mention the teaching of reading and mathematics in grades K–2 but mandates the teaching of twelve social subjects in these early grades.

Required subjects under Florida state law are Gun Safety, Consumer Education, Traffic Education, Environmental Education, Recycling of Waste, Health Education, Substance Abuse Prevention, History of Florida, Conservation of Natural Resources, Kindness to Animals, Elementary Principles of Agriculture, and the Effects of Alcohol and Intoxicating Liquors and Narcotics. Little wonder that children are not learning to read and do mathematics; there is simply no time left to teach these key subjects.

Policy makers nationwide, while imposing a similar social agenda on the early grades, have paid little or no attention to the teaching of reading and numeracy, which are the most important subjects in the curriculum.

An urgent mission in all states is for public policy makers to review the social items required in the primary grades and either eliminate this trivia or make this part of the curriculum subordinate to reading and arithmetic.

THE MATHEMATICS CURRICULUM

Historically, elementary schools in the United States have had a dual mission: (1) to prepare all students for work in an industrial and agricultural economy by teaching them basic skills; (2) to educate more thoroughly a small elite group who would go on to college and enter professional careers. Society has changed, and the percentage of students needed to work on farms and in factories has declined greatly. Yet the schools continue to misapply the curriculum of the past in educating children for the information age.

Nowhere is this misapplication of curriculum more obvious than in the field of mathematics. The world of work is becoming less routine, less manual, less mechanical, and dynamically more electronic and verbal.

The teaching of mathematics in the elementary schools

must shift from minimal mathematics for the minority and advanced mathematics for a few to a singular focus on a common core of mathematics for all students. The inference for the elementary schools is that they must provide all students with a strong foundation of mathematics for lifelong learning. Education must build continually from childhood to old age on a solid foundation provided by elementary school education. Literacy and numeracy are the linchpins of that more dynamic and versatile education.

In the learning of mathematics, relatively little is accomplished by remediation programs. Educators simply do not know how to reverse an early pattern of low achievement and failure. Repetition has not worked. The message for the schools is that the best time to learn mathematics is when it is first taught. The best way to teach mathematics is to teach it well the first time around. Pessimistic adult attitudes about mathematics have enormous influence on how well children learn this complex subject. Many adults consider mathematics as not something people actually use but something that is taught in schools and best forgotten soon afterwards. Also many adults consider mathematics to be the most painful requirement in education.

The fact that numerous adults never learned mathematics very well and succeeded without it leads to the faulty premise that large numbers of students do not need and cannot do math. The result is a spiral of lowered expectations in which poor performance in mathematics has become socially acceptable.

Another disturbing obstacle to learning mathematics is that the American public tends to assume that differentials in understanding of school mathematics are due primarily to differences in innate ability rather than differences in individual effort to learn. A consequence of this belief is that parents often accept and even expect their children to perform poorly in mathematics.

To function in today's society, mathematical literacy is becoming as essential as verbal literacy, yet the great majority of American children spend most of their school mathematics time learning only practical arithmetic. What mathematics does is contribute to literacy certain distinctive habits of mind that are of increasing importance to an informed citizenry in a technological age.

Now that mathematics, through technology, has "mathematicized" the workplace and permeated society, a complacent America cannot continue to tolerate underachievement as the norm for mathematics education. The mathematics curriculum inherited from the past, blind to the future, and bound by a tradition of minimum expectations is no longer acceptable.

Just as elementary school teachers encourage parents to read to their children at least ten minutes every day, beginning in kindergarten they should let parents know that they are expected to do math exercises with their children daily.

Schools must give whatever special assistance and support is needed to assume that all children acquire early skills and that no one falls behind.

An excellent illustration of how children see mathematics problems in different ways is the case of a teacher in a fifth grade math class who asked his students to describe the size of an acre of land. One student gave the dimensions of an acre in square feet. Another gave the dimensions in square yards. Still another defined it in meters. Finally, a student in the back of the room said, "An acre is about the size of a football field."

"Why did you say that?" the teacher asked. "Because," said the student, "everyone knows what a football field looks like."

Unlike the teacher in this illustration, too many elementary teachers make children apprehensive by having too rigid a view of mathematics with more emphasis on right answers than right thinking. Because of the fundamental importance of literacy and numeracy, reading and mathematics are the only subjects taught continuously throughout the school years. Since educators have not been successful in remediating math skills in later years, it is essential that they be well taught and well learned in the earliest years of schooling.

THE ELEMENTARY SCHOOL SCIENCE CURRICULA

Elementary school science is not well taught. The reason is the lack of preparation by elementary school teachers. The lack of formal science training makes most elementary teachers hesitate to teach science beyond what is laid out in the textbook. Instead of interesting children in science, boring textbooks convince them that science is tedious and difficult to understand. The deficiency in the training of elementary teachers to teach science has been well documented for many years, but nothing has been done about it. The outcome is disastrous for children in the nation's elementary schools.

Some 3,680,537 children born in 1982 are now entering the fourth grade. They are the graduating class of the year 2000, the class which the President and the nation's governors have said, "will be first in the world in science and mathematics achievement" (National Education Goals, 37).

It is impossible to fathom how the nation's leaders and policy makers expect to achieve this goal. As currently trained, very few elementary teachers could take advantage of a new enriched science curriculum even if it were initiated in the elementary schools. Teachers, who themselves lack confidence in their knowledge of science and hold low expectations for students, especially females and minorities, can hardly be expected to teach well. Because of unprepared teachers and a weak curriculum, students lose interest in science early in the elementary school. Textbooks which dominate elementary school science teaching are tedious and usually out of date.

Another significant problem is the absence of a science room in the public elementary schools. When a Pennsylvania school superintendent recently became interested in putting science rooms in elementary schools in his district in order to prepare students in science for the twenty-first century, he surveyed the state for a model to use as a guide. He found that there are no science rooms in any Pennsylvania public elementary schools. He did, however, find science classrooms in six private schools.

If the elementary schools are to accomplish their mission of teaching science well in order that their clientele can become "first in the world in science" within nine short years, then science must be taught in special rooms which have running water, sinks, and storage places for science equipment. Without this facility, the nation's goal for science will remain where it is today, just so much rhetoric.

The Case for Curricular Reform in Elementary Schools 123

SCIENCE MUST BE HANDS-ON

Hands-on science means just that, learning from materials of the natural world through manipulation, observation, and experimentation. It teaches children to investigate the nature of things and arrive at conclusions that are satisfying and that make sense to them.

Beginning in kindergarten, children should have hands-on experiences in science. Throughout the primary grades children need to see, touch, hear, describe, and sort the materials of science and technology. They need to question and have teachers who take their questions seriously and respond thoughtfully.

Primary age children have a natural fondness for collecting things. Teachers should capitalize on this interest and teach them to develop simple schemes for classifying objects and organisms. They must be taught to observe the changes in position and shape of the moon over a month's time. By tracking the moon's position each night at the same time and drawing pictures of the moon's changing shape, they will learn about the changes of the lunar cycle. Assigning this type of homework is also an excellent strategy for involving parents in children's learning.

Hands-on experiences should continue into intermediate grades where children do such things as learning to describe changes in the properties of water when heating, boiling, freezing, melting, or condensing.

The National Academy of Science and the Smithsonian Institution, out of concern for the absence of hands-on science programs in elementary schools, collaborated in the production of *Science for Children*, a resource book of science hands-on activities and materials. The publication is virtually a catalog of hands-on activities appropriate to primary and intermediate education.

The case for hands-on experiences is extremely powerful and has been made repeatedly by leading science scholars who advocate that science learning should be built around the big themes which hold the subject together.

In the teaching of science, a great source of support is parents. Ongoing efforts must be made to accomplish the goals of having them heavily involved. One good strategy to do this is for every elementary school to organize a science fair each year and encourage all students to enter a science project for exhibition. Schools involved in science fairs report positive and powerful feedback on the issue of parental involvement. Science fairs are excellent vehicles for teaching hands-on science.

The movement away from textbook science in the elementary schools and towards a more active curriculum is not just an American innovation. The United Kingdom, Japan, and other European and Asian nations are moving in the same direction.

After reading and mathematics, science is the next most important subject taught in the elementary schools. It must be taught efficiently and learned well. Because of insufficient efforts in the elementary schools the representation of minorities and women in careers in science is small and declining; this waste of talent is a major reason why science literacy is at a low level in our culture.

THE SLOPPY LOGIC OF SOCIAL STUDIES

One of the most illogical acts of American education is the practice of lumping history, geography, and civics together and calling the amalgamation social studies. Each of these subjects is a respectable discipline, and collectively they comprise the heart of the central responsibility of the schools: preparing students to participate in the affairs of a democratic republic.

Unfortunately, the scrambling of these three esteemed disciplines into a conglomeration called social studies has created a subject, the content of which is excessively vulnerable to the whims of textbook publishers. An examination of elementary school texts in social studies reveals that the content varies from publisher to publisher and from grade to grade. The mixing of the disciplines also gives teachers too much individual latitude in deciding what to emphasize.

The culprit responsible for merging those eminent disciplines into an amorphous subject is the National Education Association. In 1916 the NEA established a Committee on Social Studies which subsequently recommended intermingling the disciplines and calling the new subject social studies. Within the ensuing decades, school after school picked up on the recommendation with the outcome that, by about 1960, practically no schools were teaching geography, history, and government as separate disciplines. Once integrated into social studies, each discipline lost its identity and became a part of a mix of social subjects rather than three distinctive branches of knowledge. Without being certain as to what social studies should be, schools often add and delete according to the interest of the teacher.

As social studies courses exist in schools today, they are nondescript, disorganized subjects, without character and with a design and content that is vague, ill-defined, and unclear. Social studies is a textbook publisher's dream. It can and does include whatever social issues are in vogue at a particular time.

It is little wonder that American children are performing so poorly on National Assessment Tests in civics, history, and geography. The blending of the basic and important elements of culture known as history, geography, and government together into the bland subject of social studies is an aberration in need of abrogation. The results of the poor logic of merging key disciplines and inappropriately calling them social studies is now obvious.

Evidence of the ineffectiveness of the coalition can be seen on every hand. The National Assessment of Educational Progress reported in 1990 that American students demonstrated only limited understanding of the fundamental concepts of history and civics. Geography skills were described as feeble (The Nation's Report Card). Chester Finn Jr., the chairman of the NAEP's governing board, called the history and civics performance "poor" and added that together with the geography assessment, the findings suggest that the three main pillars of social studies instruction are failing (*Education Week* 2/14/90).

The assessment found little overall change from the 1986 performance, which Mr. Finn and Diane Ravitch, the distinguished professor of history at Columbia University, called "shameful." The vast majority of students at all grade levels knew trivial historical facts such as the national bird of the United States, but they were seriously lacking in their understanding of fundamental concepts. Relatively few fourth graders, the lowest grade assessed, could perform above the basic level. While 85 percent of the fourth graders could perform at the basic level, only half of the blacks and Hispanics in that grade could do so.

At the press conference releasing the results, Ina V. S. Mullis, NAEP's deputy director, noted that most students, regardless of race, performed relatively poorly on the open ended test items which asked them to use their knowledge to write answers rather than choose from multiple choice responses.

Only 6 percent of the high school seniors reached the highest level of performance, a total the evaluators called "disappointing" since that group may well represent the pool from which future leaders are drawn. Only 36 percent of the eighth graders knew that presidential candidates were nominated by party conventions. This finding was particularly discouraging since the assessment was administered during the peak of the 1986 presidential primary season.

GEOGRAPHY, A LOST SUBJECT

The assessment of what American children are learning about geography is especially disquieting. Geography has almost disappeared from the nation's elementary schools. One would naturally presume that with the world clearly shrinking in terms of technology, communications, and economic interdependence, more emphasis would be placed on the subject. Unfortunately, just the opposite is the case.

In 1990, results from the first National Assessment of how well children in school learn geography revealed "critical shortcomings," as well as the fact that a substantial number of children never even study the subject. The aforementioned Ina V. S. Mullis, deputy director of the National Assessment for Educational Progress, said the results support the public's impression that students' geographical knowledge and skills are "feeble" (*Education Week* 2/14/90).

Gilbert M. Grosvenor, president of the National Geographic Society, which helped sponsor the study, commented that the findings reflect the fact that geography is either not being taught at all in many schools or taught very poorly. It is

The Case for Curricular Reform in Elementary Schools 127

worth noting that the study found that those who had studied geography performed no better than those who did not.

Secretary of Education Lauro F. Cavazos deplored the "disturbing geography knowledge gap" and commented about the result, "Unless we place a new emphasis on the study of geography, we are passing on to our children stewardship of a world they literally do not know" (*Education Week* 2/14/90).

The average geography proficiency for demographic groups gives some clues for schools to examine as they endeavor to strengthen their geography curriculum. On average, white students outperformed Hispanic students who, in turn, outperformed black students. Males performed better than females. Students with one or two siblings performed better than those with no brothers or sisters.

As in previous NAEP assessments and numerous other studies, students with well-educated parents, access to a variety of reading materials in their homes, and with two parents or guardians living at home, performed better on geography assessment than did their less advantaged peers.

Students who reported that their mother worked, performed neither better nor worse on the assessment than those who reported that their mother did not work. Geography proficiency was higher for students who reported doing homework regularly and limiting their television viewing time.

Not only the National Assessment but a number of other studies agree on the plight of geography. A 1980 Gallup poll compared our young adults' knowledge of geography with a group of students from other countries. Our eighteen to twenty-four years-olds knew less about geography than their age mates in every other participating nation. In late 1989, a nine nation survey found that one in five young Americans (eighteen to twenty-four year-olds) could not even locate the United States on an outline map of the world. The survey reflected that only in the United States did eighteen to twenty-four year-olds know less than people fifty-five years old and over. In all of the eight other competing nations, young adults knew much more than the older ones. This finding constitutes irrefutable evidence that our schools teach much less geography than in former years.

The inferior performance of students on the geography

section of the National Assessment Test is not the only reflection that American children are not learning geography. The map-making firm Rand MacNally recently surveyed 852 elementary and secondary social studies teachers on the quality of geography instruction in the nation's schools. Almost 90 percent of the teachers surveyed rated geography instruction as poor or fair:

- 92 percent said geography illiteracy could leave U.S. citizens unable to appreciate other cultures or compete in a global market place.

- 75 percent reported that geography does not get enough attention in schools, that it is taught with history or social studies, rarely as a single subject course. A large majority of those surveyed called for more geography instruction for teachers and more emphasis in the home.

Youngsters in other countries study more geography. In England, Canada, and the Soviet Union, geography is considered one of the basic academic subjects and is required even in the high schools.

All European countries teach geography and history as separate subjects, not under the outlandish rubric of social studies. In the United States, only one in seven students takes a high school geography course. In our elementary schools the teaching of geography is hopelessly buried in the disorganized amorphous subject we call social studies.

If the elementary schools are to effectively educate citizens to live in an interconnected world, there must occur a revival of teaching this vital subject. Geography should be a pillar of the elementary school curriculum.

A major educational reform for the elementary schools is the abolition of teaching history, geography, and civics as a structureless triad under the title of social studies; each branch of knowledge should be taught individually in order that students can appreciate the full flavor and essence of the discipline.

A renewed emphasis on history, geography, and government in the elementary schools is essential to the well being of the nation and will provide students with experiences that will engage them in intellectual and academic pursuits, which after all is the main purpose of schooling.

The 1986 conference of southern governors tackled the geography issue and came out with a set of excellent recommendations appropriate to the nation's elementary schools. The conference concluded that geography is far more than knowing the names of the nation's state capitals, rivers, and mountain ranges. These topics should be studied worldwide along with the study of the world's people, their environments, and their resources. The governors' major recommendation joined the chorus of voices calling for geography to be taught as distinctive subject matter instead of a part of social studies in grades K-12.

The National Geography Bee, initiated by the *National Geographic Magazine* in 1989, has given enormous emphasis to the learning of geography. In the 1990 contest, more than three million students nationwide participated in various levels of the competition.

Television networks should broadcast the final competition in the geography bee on prime time for children's viewing as a public service. The popularity of game shows such as "Jeopardy" is proof enough that the show will be well received and enjoyed by adults as well as children.

In the distant past we could afford to divide the world into things American and non-American. This perspective no longer has credibility. We are now as dependent on other nations as they are on us, and we must begin to understand our global neighbors. The first step is to improve the teaching and understanding of geography.

HISTORY, A NEW APPROACH

The teaching of history in the elementary schools has been so deeply immersed in social studies that it is unrecognizable. Textbook publishers of social studies books have consistently succumbed to the demands of pressure groups with the result that history has been reshaped and reduced to ethnic cheerleading. In this role it has been treated as a form of social therapy whose function is to raise the self-esteem of female children and those of minority groups. Scant respect has been paid to integrity of treatment.

In its 1990 textbook adoption process, California rejected the elementary school history and social studies texts of nearly all of the publishers who submitted books for review. This action has significant implications because the state controls nearly 12 percent of the nation's textbook market. Not only did this action send a strong message to the textbook publishers, it made it difficult for the publishers to sell the rejected books in other states.

Even the textbooks from the two publishers accepted received strong criticism. Joyce King, a member of the commission, said of the newly adopted books:

> They contain distortions, inaccuracies, omissions and trivilizations (*Education Week* 8/1/90).

With the abolition of the social studies curriculum returning history to a separate discipline, the history taught to children should meet the highest standards of accuracy and veracity. It should no longer be subject to the whims of minority and women's pressure groups. Before adopting textbooks, communities should assure that history books under consideration have been carefully reviewed for content accuracy by scholarly historians.

Elementary school teachers on their part have a major role to play in reducing the sharp gaps in knowledge of history between advantaged and disadvantaged children. According to the National Assessment for Education Progress, most history instruction is presently characterized by reading from textbooks. More attention must be given to reading primary source materials, speeches and documents, engaging in group discussions, and writing. These are well-accepted strategies for interesting and exciting ways to teach history.

Current social studies textbooks are so dull that no one would read them voluntarily. In fact very few members of state textbook adoption committees take time to read them. Instead they use as their guide a checklist provided by the department of education. This criteria deals with such things as whether the book has adequate pictures and a recent publication date.

The textbook reviewers should be required to (1) read the books and (2) make use of reviews by scholars, teachers, and historians. Schools need to become less textbook oriented, and the textbooks selected should be more accurate and of higher quality.

HOMEWORK: A VIABLE RESPONSE TO REFORM

One way for teachers to respond to public demands for higher standards and more rigor in the elementary school is to assign homework regularly beginning in kindergarten. The goal is to motivate younger children and foster positive attitudes and habits about school work. Consequently, assignments should be short, related to materials commonly found in the home, and designed to give students successful experiences.

The reasons for homework assignments are threefold:

- Boost achievement.
- Develop student initiative.
- Help children see that learning happens in places other than the schools.

Principals should discuss homework policies with their staff, clarify the purpose of homework, and carefully monitor the practice to assure that assignments are having the desired effect on students' motivation and attitudes. How much and what kind of homework are questions which not only serve the interest of children but act as a communication between the school and home.

SPECIAL EDUCATION

States need to take strong action to curb the growth of special education costs. With the expense of educating handicapped children at two and a half times the cost of educating non-handicapped children, there is increasing concern that 10 to 12 percent of the children are siphoning away money from the majority.

The major issue is school cheating by placing troublesome but non-handicapped students in special education programs. The problem here is that inept teachers, who are unable to deal with the wide range of students in regular classrooms, arrange to have troublesome children labeled with an educational handicap and transferred to special education. The various states' departments of education have been lax in not targeting school districts which allow this practice and witholding their funds for cheating. Strong and vigorous action should be taken by all states to eliminate this malpractice.

The other side of the coin is the injustice done to many children identified as learning disabled but who are not actually handicapped. Their only misfortune is that they have had contact with inept teachers.

The tragedy of special education is not that it is excessively costly, litigious, misguided, or ineffective. Its misfortune is being used by incompetent teachers as a vehicle for getting rid of competent but troublesome children.

CHAPTER 10

The Case for and Against Educational Technology: An Elusive Reform

Elementary school educators have an extremely poor track record in adapting educational technology to classroom use. During the late 1930's, when radio was at its height, educators in thousands of elementary schools in the eastern part of the United States put a radio in every classroom so the schools could begin the day with the Columbia School of the Air. This was a radio program which was broadcast every morning at 9:00 A. M. from New York City. This innovation was short-lived, and schools soon discarded radio technology as a learning medium and returned to the traditional teacher and chalkboard.

History repeated itself in the late 1950's when school districts all across the country equipped every classroom with a television set in anticipation of using television as a major teaching tool. The Ford Foundation even outfitted an airplane with instructional programs and kept it flying around the middle of the country beaming educational television signals to all the classrooms in the Midwest. After the initial burst of enthusiasium and millions of dollars in expenditures, the television sets were abandoned by the schools and the Ford Foundation grounded its airplane.

History repeated itself for the third time in the early 1980's when elementary schools rushed to purchase computers for every classroom. Many of these computers are now either obsolete or stored on a shelf somewhere.

But in spite of these setbacks, the idea of improving instruction through the use of technology persists and the case for technology in the classroom has not yet been decided. While computers certainly have not lived up to their once-heralded ability to "revolutionize" education, the jury is still out.

As we move into the second decade of computer use, educators and researchers can benefit from the conclusion reached by Jess House of the University of Toledo, "Our review of the first decade of the use of micro-computers in the classroom reveals that mistakes have been made and promises left unfulfilled" (John Hopkins University 1989).

The *Wall Street Journal* noted that to conclude that computers have "transformed" or "revolutionized" education would be misleading. The *Journal* commented: "Even after spending more than $2 billion on an estimated 1.7 million personal computers, educators are hard pressed to spot the heralded revolution in the schoolhouse" (3/6/89).

After examining the evidence of computer use in schools, it is now clear that "general widespread computer use has not produced measurable gains in learning."

What does the mixed review from researchers imply for instructional computing? The visionaries continue to look off into the hazy future while the people who are responsible for day-to-day learning in the classroom face a critical challenge in either doing nothing or determining an acceptable level of risk taking that will be supported by the local community.

So, what are the schools doing about educational technology? The present status is one of educators still searching for hard evidence that computers can substantially improve learning.

Results from recent studies attempting to determine the effectiveness of educational technology are often criticized for being either inconclusive or contradictory to previous research. In addition, those looking for widespread gains say that much of the reported success has been isolated and anecdotal, and it has been more often focused on social and psychological benefits than academic achievement. Certainly, at this time there is little hard evidence that the use of computers in the elementary school dramatically increases academic learning.

While the number of computers in public schools is increasing each year, many educators question whether or not the technology is actually having any impact on teaching methods and course content.

There are several issues which have hindered the use and spread of technology. The first and foremost obstacle in most schools systems is that policy concerning the use of technology first must be negotiated with the teachers' unions through the collective bargaining process. Secondly, before implementing programs, school decision makers must grapple with issues as basic as the school system's philosophical foundations.

Another significant inhibiting issue to success is the way in which school systems often get off on the wrong foot with the use of computers by starting out teaching children to play computer games. The outcome has been that many schools never get past the game playing stage.

An internal issue needing a solution is the method by which most school districts acquire computers. The process is often done in a hodgepodge, piecemeal fashion, rather than through thoughtful planning and purchasing. Frequently schools end up with three or four different types and an array of incompatible software.

A survey of 773 of the country's largest school districts, conducted in the spring of 1988, (Isabelle Bruder 1988) found that more than half the school districts focused on computer literacy and instructional computing. This was surprising since the evidence is clear that best results are obtained from a comprehensive integration of both instructional and management technology.

A troubling issue that frequently arises is the absence of equity in computer use in schools. When research considers the differences in students using computers along ethnic, gender, ability, and socio-economic lines, generally boys and better students are found to use computers more than other groups. Students from affluent school districts are more likely to have access to a computer at school than students in poorer districts.

The results of these initial studies have raised important questions about equity in school computer use. Computer equity should be determined by how well schools are using computers to meet the educational needs of each child, not by guaranteeing equal time on a computer for each student.

Before schools can successfully develop the full potential of the computer, it is essential to first examine what it is that the computer is purported to do well educationally. One thing it does very well is drill. Its capacity for extreme patience can provide excellent drill and practice exercises. The question becomes, "Is that what children in school ought to be doing?" What the schools should be about is problem solving and the development of higher order thinking and learning skills. Present software does not accommodate this type of teaching and learning.

At this time word processing is the best application for computers at the elementary school level, especially when the teaching of revision as part of the process of writing is emphasized. In order for schools to do this well, they must acquire the necessary hardware and software to create a word processing laboratory. In language arts it is now clear that word processing is an excellent technique for the teaching of writing skills to elementary school students.

Next to word processing, the best application in elementary schools is the use of the computer as a teaching medium. This enhances the use of the chalkboard and is accomplished by connecting one computer to a large screen monitor for effective and more efficient classroom instruction. In this configuration, computers are useful in science, social studies, and mathematics. Use of this technique requires teacher inservice in effective questioning strategies with appropriate feedback as an outcome.

In mathematics problem solving, complex thinking is a fairly easy outcome. The computer's ability to take in data, save it, and provide immediate feedback creates an environment of continual hypothesizing, testing, and refining.

Databases have little application to the elementary school because most of the children do not have the ability to select data according to criteria. While databases have potential at the secondary school level, students' understanding of their power may be too limited to be worthwhile in the elementary school. A common mistake that educators have made is to water down material for elementary school students, rather than leave it for more mature students who are developmentally ready for it. The spreadsheet is a powerful mathematics modeling tool, but its use requires abstract understanding of formulas and is more appropriate at the secondary level.

The promise of computers and other technologies is the potential to push back the traditional frontiers of cognition and learning. They also advance the notion that technology can make possible the kinds of intellectual endeavor for which measures of achievement have not yet been invented. Once schools learn how to adapt technology to the learning process, the medium offers a special promise to make our schools more productive learning environments. It also has the potential of transforming the entire landscape of education in the United States.

So what should elementary schools be doing about the use of computers? Since the state of the art in elementary education is still close to genesis, schools should move forward, but discreetly and with caution. To rush out and purchase a computer for every student at this stage of the game is foolhardy for two reasons: (1) the software has simply not kept up with the hardware, and good programs are few and far between; (2) since the hardware is changing rapidly, almost anything that the school buys at this point will soon be obsolete.

The most prudent course is to invest with moderation in order to keep up and experiment with emerging improved software. Secondly, make certain that teachers are trained to use computers and encourage teachers to experiment with promising programs.

A distinct roadblock at this point is the miserable failure of colleges of education to prepare beginning teachers in the use of technology. This means that school districts must pick up this task and assure that all of the teaching staff is knowledgeable both in the use of computers and about the most promising software available in their fields.

Better use of technology in education, while still an unfulfilled promise, must continue to be considered as a potential source for a quantum leap in student achievement.

The evidence is clear that the present system of the teacher, the chalkboard, and twenty-five students has reached the limits of its productivity. After a massive effort, perhaps this system can be improved by another 5 percent, but that is about all. What is required is a revolutionary new approach to teaching and learning. Hopefully, emerging new hardware and software and different ways of integrating computer activities with other components of instruction will profoundly affect the direction and outcomes of student achievement.

While we continue to search for a body of evidence about conditions and circumstances for using technology to improve learning outcomes, we must face the reality that we simply are not there yet. Perhaps the best analysis of the present status of technology in the classroom is found in a report from the Center for Research on Elementary and Middle Schools at the John Hopkins University. This research concludes that, "Existing evidence of computer effectiveness is very scanty and existing studies provide little guidance for schools to decide how to use computers for instruction" (*The Impact of Computer Use on Children's Learning 1989*).

Still, proponents of educational technology in the elementary schools argue that the delivery system in use has become obsolete. After thirty years of tinkering with different techniques and styles of teaching, knowledge is delivered in much the same fashion as at the turn of the century.

Added to the ineffectiveness of the conventional classroom with one teacher to twenty-five or thirty students is the inadequacy of elementary school textbooks. Curricula, purchased from textbook publishers, have shown little if any improvement despite decades of dissatisfaction from schools, parent groups, school boards, and legislators.

Beginning with grade two, textbooks become repetitive and by about grade five excessively so. At the seventh grade level, roughly 50 percent of material covered in school texts is redundant. The outcome is that conventional textbooks fail to introduce enough new material to keep students challenged or even interested. The promise of technology is that it can make traditional materials obsolete by replacing them with interesting and challenging learning situations.

> An analysis of opinions about the schools and technology reflects that, the technological gap between the school environment and the real world is growing so wide, so fast that the educational experience is at risk of becoming not merely unproductive but utterly irrelevant to the nation's future needs (Morgan 1989).

For nearly a decade, two huge technology firms have vied for control of the school market, IBM and Apple. Most educators believe that IBM has already conceded the market to Apple; however, "Writing to Read," IBM's major initiative, continues to be popular among both educators and policy makers. While governors in a number of states have mandated "Writing to Read" in the primary schools, many educators warn that the popularity of the program is due more to the ingenious and aggressive marketing of IBM than to any proof that the program is educationally effective.

Despite increasing reliance by the elementary school on the IBM package as a way to boost skills in reading and writing, critics contend that there is not one shred of evidence to prove that it is more effective than traditional and less costly approaches to teaching reading and writing. As long as no research exists to support sweeping technological changes in teaching and learning, no decisions should be made at the policy level.

The enormous public pressure to which the elementary schools are being subjected to use computers is generated by the fact that the United States has the dubious distinction of owning almost half of the computers on the planet. The *Washington Post* estimates that of the eighty-one million computers in the world, forty million are in the United States (4/19/90).

With computers being this broadly used throughout American society, it is little wonder that technology advocates insist that technology can solve the problems of the nation's schools.

But with all of its promise, results from educational technology do not just appear with the waving of a magic wand.

The eminent historian Diane Ravitch of Columbia University put the issue in perspective with the warning that in social studies there are periods of historical significance that are not addressed by the electronic media. She cautions that what is worth teaching may not be available yet in a high tech medium (Education Week 1/24/90).

While schools have become bogged down over the issues of which computers to buy, where to put them, and how to schedule their use, the real concern is how do they fit into the curriculum and whether they can improve learning. Implementing programs solely because they engage students' attention more quickly than print media does students a distinct disservice.

The promise of technology is a new era of self-paced learning which will allow elementary schools to better address the needs of an increasingly diverse student population nearly half of which is at risk. New systems which will enable the schools to focus on the development of skills and student achievement by this hard-to-teach group will be a welcome addition to elementary school education.

With educational efficiency at capacity and below expectations, schools should vigorously be searching for a new instructional delivery model. However, they must guard against being carried away by wild-eyed visionaries who conceive of sophisticated technology revolutionizing the nation's kindergartens.

The ultimate decision on the place of technology in elementary school classrooms can be decided only on the basis of its effectiveness in improving student achievement. At present technology, particularly the use of computers, remains an elusive reform.

CHAPTER 11

Executive Summary of Recommendations for Elementary School Reform

The major education issue before the nation is the absence of a comprehensive plan to reform education in grades K–6. A series of actions designed to improve the quality of education at all levels of the elementary school should be implemented with a sense of urgency.

The makers of public policy have handled the elementary schools with kid gloves in the past, apparently assuming that this level of schooling is up to standard, but nothing could be further from the truth. Policy makers must now concentrate on reforming this area by initiating new and stronger leadership, a more demanding curriculum, higher quality of teaching, and far more rigorous standards for students.

The intent of reforming elementary schools is to make the nation's schools places of tougher standards, higher goals, and greater expectations. Education must no longer be a service rendered by school boards in the same way that cities provide electricity and water.

Bold action is required in the effort to accomplish improved outcomes in student achievement. Minimum outcomes expected: (1) all non-handicapped children will be reading with proficiency by the end of the first grade; (2) all students will be at or above grade level in each year of schooling. These and other student outcomes should be specified by policy makers at the state level and straightforward instructions issued to assure that they are achieved.

Implementation of elementary school reforms is largely a matter of will on the part of state and local education authorities. Within this context the following reforms are appropriate for early implementation:

- State policy makers establish clearly prescribed student outcomes for schools and direct school districts to achieve them. An outcome of the highest priority is to require school boards to guarantee that following six years at one of their elementary schools, all non-handicapped students entering middle school will be at or above grade level.

- If a school district is unable to attain the student outcomes specified, then its school board members are disqualified from filing for reelection or reappointment to another term.

- Superintendents are employed for a maximum of two years with the caveat that further employment be based upon student outcomes. Automatic dismissal occurs when expected outcomes are not reached. Exceptions may not be made.

- Elementary school principals are employed for a two year period, and reemployment is based upon student achievement. When achievement goals are not reached, the principal becomes ineligible for another administrative position for three years.

- If a teacher's students fail to meet the expected outcomes at the end of a school year, the teacher is placed on probation and transferred to another teaching situation. The second time this teacher's students fail to meet anticipated outcomes, his or her service is discontinued.

- Certificates of excellence, higher than ordinary salary increases, and other honors and awards of recognition are awarded to teachers whose students achieve substantially above the expected outcomes.

- Differentiate teachers' salaries and base them on the results teachers achieve rather than seniority.

Executive Summary of Recommendations for Reform

- Business and industry endow chairs for distinguished teaching in the elementary schools modeled after professional chairs in colleges and universities.
- Tenure, the practice of giving lifetime contracts of employment to teachers and administrators, is eliminated from school law in all states.
- Policy makers recognize that the early years of education are the most important in the eduction ladder and shift resources from the top heavy end of the education structure to early years.
- The social studies curiculum which combines geography, history, and government is abolished and each of these disciplines taught as a separate entity.
- Geography is taught as a separate subject each year of elementary schooling beginning with kindergarten.
- History is taught as a distinct discipline each year of elementary schooling beginning with grade one.
- Kindergarten children are helped to achieve at a substantially faster rate of intellectual activity.
- The emphasis in the kindergarten curriculum is shifted from social and developmental activities to the teaching of reading and mathematics.
- In places where kindergarten operates as a half day activity, the time is lengthened to a full day.
- A higher priority is placed on the teaching of reading and mathematics in kindergarten through grade three.
- All children are able to read with proficiency by the end of the first grade.
- Each of the nation's elementary schools completes an in-depth study of the demography of students in prekindergarten and grades K–6. The data is used to design and implement extended day schools and provide the best possible services and education for all children.

- Lengthen the elementary school day until 5:30 P.M. to (1) increase learning and (2) accommodate the large numbers of children coming from homes in which both parents are in the workforce (45 percent) and the children from single parent homes (22 percent). The program focus in the added time should be on the optimization of technology, reading skills, language skills, numeracy, and science.

- Where many children are living below the poverty level with a single parent, schools must pick up and teach in school based early childhood education the "hidden curriculum" which family life has imparted to children in the past.

- Eliminate remediation in the elementary school by not allowing children to fall behind in learning. Personal tutoring by peers, high school students, volunteers, and paid staff is brought to bear at the time the child has difficulty. If necessary, children falling behind attend school on Saturdays.

- Elementary schools become more sensitive and responsive to changing family lifestyles.

- Re-engage families in the education of elementary school children.

- Parents are able to select the school of their choice, be it public or private, and the money follows the student.

- Stress character formation before skill acquisition in prekindergarten early childhood programs.

- Expand school based prekindergarten programs to accommodate all poor and economically disadvantaged four-year-olds.

- Discontinue the practice of classifying an excessive number of students as having learning disabilities for no other reasons than to obtain increased funding and the inability of inept teachers to deal with troublesome students.

- Eliminate grade retention in K–6. Promote all children but follow through with continuing assistance and support.

- Abolish grade levels in grade K–3.

Executive Summary of Recommendations for Reform

- Strengthen science teaching in grades three through six using a "hands-on" curriculum.

- Establish higher academic standards for admission to teacher training.

- Improve preparation of teachers by the colleges of education in the use of technology in the classroom.

- Reform colleges of education around two issues:
  —What is essential for beginning teachers to know?
  —What teacher skills and abilities are effective?
  Then reduce them to department status in the College of Liberal Arts.

- Open teacher certification to any teacher with a bachelor's degree without the requirement of specific education courses. Immerse new teachers in eight weeks of intensive training in school classrooms.

- Business leaders seeking an active role in school reform are urged to stress investment in the early years versus the later ones.

- Elementary school policy advises parents to substitute reading, instructive hobbies, and athletics for television viewing, which should be limited to a maximum of one hour a day, or eliminated altogether.

- Administrators do away with the practice of assigning one teacher to twenty or thirty students and instead have all teachers at the same grade level work as a team. This team of teachers should remain with the same group of students for three years.

- Abolish use of a checklist by local textbook adoption committees and require committee members to read the books under consideration. Reviews of the books by scholars should be available to committee members.

- Prudently invest in and experiment with technology in order to find a better delivery system.

- All veteran teachers are trained to use computers and encouraged to experiment with promising programs.

- Expand the use of technology as part of the strategy to achieve an increase in learning outcomes.
- Initiate performance outcomes for every school and every student and take whatever action is necessary to see that they are achieved.
- Give top priority to improving learning outcomes for minorities in the early grades and making their achievement equal to that of non-minorities.
- Target children from low income families and initiate effective intervention in the form of nuturing and the instruction necessary to prepare them for a difficult future.
- By the end of grade three every child is able to read with comprehension, write with clarity, compute with accuracy, and speak effectively. If these skills are well formed, each child can be assured of satisfactory performance in the intermediate and middle school.
- States issue report cards annually on each school district and each school in the state. The elementary school annual report card is published in every newspaper and includes the following items:
  —Expenditures per pupil
  —Percentage of attendance
  —Percentage of student mobility
  —Standardized test scores on reading and mathematics
- Beginning with grade three all students are taught a second language.

Although *A Nation At Risk* was published in 1983 with its alarming prediction of catastrophe if schools do not improve, gains in learning have not occurred. While a lot of noise has been made about reform in schools, the quality of education for children is no better.

For eight years educators have ignored warning signals. They have been unwilling or unable to respond to ubiquitous demands for an increase in student achievement. The lack of response from educators to do something about the shortfall in learning has created another crisis with which the battered education system must now contend. A weary public, upset about higher taxes and mediocre school performance, is losing its enthusiasum for providing the additional resources to support school improvement as it has in the past few years.

Admittedly, educators have done some reform, but at best the effort has been tinkering by implementing haphazard and piecemeal changes such as giving parents some choice of schools and teachers more power to make decisions. These are peripheral reforms which will not give the nation the gains in learning for which it is yearning. After eight years of ominous predictions, educators continue to tiptoe around the issue of extensive reform while the clock keeps ticking. They seem unaware that the nation is moving from a local to a national view of education. What is happening was best described by Emily O. Wurtz, a researcher in the U.S. Department of Education:

> The basis for judging school performance is shifting from local satisfaction based on local criteria to the achievement of student outcomes which can be objectively measured and compared on an international basis (*Education Week* 4/25/90).

The recommendations in this report are directed at achieving substantial and imposing gains in student outcomes. They are drastic, extreme, and uncompromising.

The substance of the report is to echo the warning tremors of the educational policy earthquake which is on the way. The time is fast approaching when teachers and administrators will be employed and judged solely on the extent to which they boost student outcomes in achievement. Only then will the nation attain the large gains in learning which are necessary for our continued role as a world economic power. In the meantime the nation continues to search for the right mix of educational wisdom, standards of performance, and an able cadre of educators to lead the reform movement.

References

Bruder, Isabelle, *Eighth Annual Survey of the States* (1988).
Bruner, Jerome, *Process of Education* (Cambridge: Harvard University Press, 1963).
Colorado State Department of Education, *Bulletin on Innovation* (1990).
Coleman, James, *Schools, Families and Children*, Ryerson Lecture, University of Chicago (1985).
Coons, Robert and Sugarman, Stephen, *Education by Choice: The Case for Family Control* (University of Chicago Press, 1978).
Daedalus, "Education of Teachers" (Fall 1981).
Economic Policy Institute, *Shortchanging Education: How U.S. Spending on Grades K–12 Lags Behind Other Nations* (1990).
Education Week "NAEP Results in Reading, Writing, Show Few Gains" (1/17/90).
Education Week, "Study Puts U.S. Near Bottom in School Spending" (1/24/90).
Education Week, "Reading Study Comes Up Short, Lawmakers Assert" (2/7/90).
Education Week, "The Need For Better Data on Education" (2/7/90).
Education Week, "Aiming for a Definition of Literacy" (2/14/90).
Education Week, "NAEP Geography Assessment Finds Knowledge Gaps" (2/14/90).
Education Week, "Single Definition of Restructuring Remains Elusive" (2/21/90).
Education Week, "From a Great Debate to a Full-Scale War: Reading Dispute Over Teaching Reading Heats Up" (3/21/90).
Education Week, "Teacher Programs Urged to Shift Emphasis from Research to Training" (4/25/90).
Education Week, "Education Officials Reconsider Policies On Grade Retention" (5/16/90).

Education Week, "States Take Stock of Math Programs in Wake of NAEP Results" (6/19/91).
Education Week, "California Rejects Most History Texts Submitted" (8/1/90).
Education Week, "Why Sesame Street is Bad News for Reading" (9/19/90).
Education Week, "Controversial Education Proposals Give Wisconsin Governor Extra Edge" (10/31/90).
Education Week, "Goodlad Teacher Education Study Calls for Centers of Pedagogy" (10/24/90).
Ferguson, Ronald, *Challenge: A Journal of Research on Black Men* Vol. 2 #1 (Morehouse College, Atlanta, Georgia, May 1991).
Florida Commission on Schools Report (Tallahassee, Florida, 1989).
Florida State Board of Education Minutes (Tallahassee, Florida, 1/20/81).
Florida School Law. (1991)
Goodlad, John, *A Place Called School* (McGraw-Hill, 1984).
Goodlad, John, (Speech to American Association of Colleges of Teachers Education 4/12/90).
Head Start Association, *The Nation's Pride, A Nation's Challenge* (4/18/90).
Healey, Jane M. *Endangered Minds: Why Our Children Don't Think* (Simon and Schuster, 1991).
Hunt, J. McVicker, *Intelligence and Experience* (Simon Schuster, 1961).
John Hopkins University *Impact of Computer Use on Children's Learning* (Pamphlet, 1989).
Massachusetts State Board of Education Minutes (Boston, Mass., April 1990).
Minnesota School Law (1990).
Morgan, Robert, Florida Commission on School Reform (Minutes Oct. 1989).
National Assessment of Education Progress: *The Reading Report Card* (1967–1988).
National Assessment of Education Progress, *State Mathematics Achievement* (1991).
National Center for Education *Survey* (1990).
National Center for Health *Statistics* vol. 39 #4 1988.
National Commission on Excellence, *A Nation At Risk* (1983).
National Governors' Association Minutes (1989).
National Governors' Association Minutes (1990).
National Governors' Association, "Educating America" (1990, 37–38).
New York State Board of Regents Minutes (Albany, New York, 5/90).
The New York Times, "Educating Teachers" (10/6/90).

References

Pipo, Chris, Research Director Education Commission of the States, Conversation with Author (June 1991).
Report of the Commission on Reading *Becoming a Nation of Readers* (Government Printing Office, 1985).
Smithsonian Institution, *Reading Is Fundamental*, (Government Printing Office, 1989).
U.S. Department of Education School Survey (1967).
Wall Street Journal, "Schools and Technology" (4/24/90).
Wall Street Journal, "Homeschooling" (10/10/90).
White House Press Release (2/26/90).
White House Press Release (3/4/90).

Index

Academic contests, 101
American Academy of Pediatrics, 58
Antiquated Educational Laws, 107
At-risk syndrome, 24

Census Bureau Data, 20
Change model, 44
Charter schools, 14
Choice, 64
Colleges of education, 108
Connecticut's Plan, 83
Corporate America, 102
Curricular reform, 115

Debate over reading, 51
Decline in learning, 105

Educational technology, 133
Education Summit, 7

Geography, 126
Grade retention, 31
Guaranteed achievement, 75

History, 129
Home schooling, 59
Homework, 131

Improving students' outcomes, 91
Inflated test scores, 50

Lengthening school days, 67

Magnet schools, 96

Mathematics curriculum, 119
Minority learning, 95

National Commission on Excellence, 1
National goals, 9
National Governors' Assn., 88

Parent involvement, 101
Performance contracts, 112
Principal as CEO, 80

Recommendations for reform, 141
Reform strategy, 13
Researchers and readiness, 48
Retention effects, 33

School district report cards, 86
School diversity, 64
Science curricula, 121
Sesame Street, 56
Special education, 131
State intervention, 89
State policy on principals, 79

Teachers' unions, 82
Team teaching, 43
Television and children, 55
Testing, 91
Theme centered curricula, 71
Types of magnet schools, 98

Uninterrupted learning, 35

Whittle Schools, 16